THE
PILGRIM'S
PROGRESS

JOHN BUNYAN

British Library Cataloguing in Publication Data
A record for this book is available from the British Library

ISBN: 978-1-78397-214-2

Designed by Pete Barnsley (CreativeHoot.com)

Printed in the UK

Evangelical Press, (EP Books), an imprint of 10Publishing
Unit C, Tomlinson Road, Leyland, PR25 2DY, England

Email: epbooks@10ofthose.com
Website: www.epbooks.org

CONTENTS

"*Dearly beloved, I beseech you as strangers and pilgrims — abstain from fleshly lusts which war against the soul.*" 1 Peter 2:11

"*These all died in faith, not having received the promises, but having seen them afar off were assured of them, embraced them and confessed that they were strangers and pilgrims on the earth.*" Hebrews 11:13

"*Enter by the narrow gate; for wide is the gate and broad is the way that leads to destruction — and there are many who go in by it. Because narrow is the gate and difficult is the way which leads to life — and there are few who find it.*" Matthew 7:13-14

CHAPTER 1

THE CITY OF DESTRUCTION

As I walked through the wilderness of this world, I came upon a certain place, where there was a den, and I laid down in that place to sleep. And as I slept, I dreamed a dream. I dreamed, and, behold, I saw a man clothed with rags, standing with his face turned away from his own house, with a Book in his hand, and a great burden upon his back. I looked, and saw him open the Book, and read therein; and as he read, he wept and trembled! And not being able to contain himself any longer, he broke out with a lamentable cry, saying, *"What shall I do?"*

In this plight, therefore, he went home, and restrained himself as long as he could, so that his wife and children would not notice his great distress. But he could not be silent for long, because his trouble only increased. Therefore at length, he spoke his mind to his wife and children, and thus he began to talk to them: *"O my dear wife, and you, my dear children, I am undone, because of this burden which lies heavily upon me! Moreover, I am certainly informed, that this city of ours will be burned with fire from Heaven! In that fearful catastrophe, both myself, with you, my wife, and you, my sweet babes shall come to miserable ruin, unless some way of escape can be found, whereby we may be delivered."*

At this, his family was greatly bewildered, not that they believed what he had said to them was true, but because they thought that his mind had become deranged.

Therefore, as it was drawing towards night, and hoping that sleep might settle his brains, with all haste they put him to bed. But the night was as troublesome to him as the day, and instead of sleeping, he spent it in sighs and tears! When the morning came, they inquired how he felt. He told them, *"Worse and worse!"* He then commenced to talk to them again, but they began to be hardened. They also thought to drive away his derangement, by harsh and cruel conduct toward him. Sometimes they would deride him, sometimes they would chide him, and sometimes they would simply ignore him.

Therefore he began to withdraw himself to his room to pray for, and pity them, and also to comfort his own misery. He would also walk solitarily in the fields, sometimes reading, and sometimes praying. And thus for several days, he spent his time in this manner.

Now I saw in my dream, while he was walking in the fields, that he was reading in his Book, as was his habit. Being greatly distressed in his mind as he read, he burst out, as he had done before, crying, *"What shall I do to be saved?"*

I saw also, that he looked this way and that way, as if he wanted to run. Yet he stood still, because, as I perceived, he could not tell which way to go. I looked then, and saw a man named Evangelist coming towards him, who asked, *"Why are you crying out?"*

He answered, *"Sir, I realize, by the Book in my hand that I am condemned to die, and after that to come to judgment. And I find that I am not willing to do the first, nor able to do the second."*

Then Evangelist said, *"Why are you not willing to die, since this life is attended with so many troubles?"*

The man answered, *"Because I fear that this burden upon my back will sink me lower than the grave, and I shall fall into Hell! And, Sir, if I am not fit to die, then I am sure that I am not fit to go to judgment, and from thence to execution! My thoughts about these things make me cry out!"*

Then Evangelist said, *"If this is your condition, why do you stand still?"*

He answered, *"Because I do not know where to go!"*

Then Evangelist gave him a parchment scroll, on which was written, *"Flee from the wrath to come!"*

The man therefore, reading it, looked very sincerely upon Evangelist, and asked, *"Where must I flee?"*

Then Evangelist, pointing with his finger over a very wide field, said, *"Do you see yonder narrow-gate?"*

The man answered, *"No."*

Evangelist replied, *"Do you see yonder shining light?"*

He said, *"I think I do."*

Then Evangelist said, *"Keep that light in your eye, and go directly to it and then you shall see the gate; at which, when you knock, you shall be told what you must do."*

So I saw in my dream, that the man began to run. Now, he had not run far from his own door, before his wife and children, seeing him depart, began to shout after him to return. But the man put his fingers in his ears, and ran on, crying, *"Life! life! Eternal life!"*

So he did not look behind him, but fled towards the middle of the plain.

CHAPTER 2

OBSTINATE AND PLIABLE

T he neighbors also came out to see him run. As he ran, some mocked, others threatened, and some cried after him to return. Among those who did so, were two who were resolved to fetch him back by force. The name of the one was Obstinate and the name of the other was Pliable. Now by this time, the man had gone a good distance away from them; but they were resolved to pursue him, and in a little while, they caught up with him.

Then the man said, *"Neighbors, why have you come?"*

They answered, *"To persuade you to go back with us!"*

But he said, *"That cannot be! You dwell in the City of Destruction, the place where I also was born. I see that, sooner or later, dying there, we will sink lower than the grave, into a place which burns with fire and brimstone! Think, good neighbors, and come along with me!"*

"What!" said Obstinate, *"and leave our friends and our comforts behind us?"*

"Yes," said Christian, for that was his name, *"because all that you shall forsake, is not worthy to be compared with a little of what I am seeking to enjoy. And if you will go along with me, and persevere, you shall fare as well as I myself. For there, where I am going, is more than enough and to spare. Come along and see that my words are true!"*

"What are the things which you seek," asked Obstinate, *"since you are leaving all the world to find them?"*

Christian answered, *"I am seeking an inheritance which can never perish, spoil or fade, safe and reserved in Heaven, to be bestowed, at the appointed time, on those who diligently seek it. Read it so, if you will, here in my Book!"*

"Nonsense!" cried Obstinate, *"Away with your Book! Will you go back with us, or not?"*

"No, not I!" said Christian, *"Because I have put my hand to the plough and will not turn back!"*

"Come, then, neighbor Pliable," said Obstinate, *"let us go home without him. There are too many of these silly fools who, when they get a crazy thought in their head, are wiser in their own eyes, than seven men who can think reasonably!"*

"Do not revile him," said Pliable, *"if what Christian says is true, then the things which he follows after, are better than ours and my heart is inclined to go with him!"*

"What!" bellowed Obstinate, *"More fools still! Take my word, and go back with me. Who knows where such a foolish fellow will lead you? Come back! Come back and be wise!"*

"No!" said Christian, *"rather come along with me, Obstinate! We will receive such things as I spoke of and many more indescribable blessings besides. If you do not believe me, then read here in my Book! These truths are all confirmed by the blood of Him who wrote it!"*

"Well, neighbor Obstinate," said Pliable, *"I intend to go along with this good man and to cast in my lot with him."*

Then Pliable turned to Christian and asked, *"Do you know the way to this glorious place?"*

Christian replied, *"I have been directed by a man whose name is Evangelist, to hasten to the narrow-gate ahead of us, where we shall receive instructions about the Way."*

"Come then, good Christian, let us be going!" said Pliable. Then they began to travel along together.

"And I will go back to my place!" said Obstinate. *"I will be no companion to such misled foolish fellows!"*

Now I saw in my dream, that Obstinate went back, and Christian and Pliable went along towards the narrow-gate, conversing together.

"Neighbor Pliable," said Christian, *"I am glad you were persuaded to go along with me. Had Obstinate but felt what I have felt, of the powers and terrors of unseen realities, he would not have so easily turned back."*

Pliable replied, *"Tell me further, Christian, what are these glorious things, and how are they to be enjoyed?"*

"I can better understand them with my mind than speak of them with my tongue!" said Christian. *"But since you are desirous to know, I will describe them to you, from my Book."*

"And do you think that the words of your Book are really true?" asked Pliable.

"Yes, absolutely, for it was written by Him who cannot lie!" answered Christian.

"What are these glorious things of which you speak?" questioned Pliable.

"There is an eternal kingdom, and everlasting life to be given to us, where we will dwell forever!" replied Christian.

"And what else is there?" asked Pliable.

"We will be given crowns of glory, and garments which shine like the sun!"

"This is wonderful!" exclaimed Pliable. *"And what else will there be?"*

"There will be no more crying, nor sorrow, for He who reigns over that place will wipe all tears from our eyes!" responded Christian.

"And what company shall we have there?" Pliable inquired.

Christian answered, *"There we shall be with Seraphim and Cherubim, creatures which will dazzle your eyes to look upon! There, also, you shall meet with thousands, and tens of thousands who have gone ahead of us to that Place. They are all loving and holy, each one fully accepted by God, and standing in His presence. In a word, there we shall dwell with all the redeemed people of God, having golden crowns and golden harps! We shall also see those who, for the love which they bore to the Savior, were cut in pieces, burned in the flames, eaten by beasts, or drowned in the seas. They are all perfect, and clothed with immortality!"*

"Just hearing of this, is enough to ravish one's heart!" said Pliable. *"How are these things to be enjoyed and how can we obtain them?"*

Christian responded, *"The Lord, the Governor of that country, has recorded in His Book that if we are truly willing to have it He will bestow it upon us freely."*

"Well, my good companion," said Pliable, *"I am thrilled to hear of these things! Come, let us quicken our pace!"*

"I cannot go so fast as I would," answered Christian, *"because of this burden which is on my back!"*

CHAPTER 3

THE SWAMP OF DESPOND

Now I saw in my dream, that just as they had ended this talk, they drew near to a very miry swamp, which was in the midst of the plain; and they, not paying attention, fell suddenly into the bog. The name of the swamp was Despond. Here, therefore, they wallowed for a time, being greatly smeared with filth. Christian, because of the burden which was on his back, began to sink in the mire.

Then Pliable cried out, *"Ah! Christian, where are we now?"*

"Truly," said Christian, *"I do not know!"*

Being offended, Pliable angrily said to his companion, *"Is this the happiness you have told me of? If we have such trouble at our first setting out, what may we expect before our journey's end? If I can get out of here with my life you can have your noble country without me!"*

And with that, Pliable, after a desperate struggle got out of the mire on that side of the swamp which was nearest to his own house. So away he went and Christian saw him no more.

So Christian was left in the Swamp of Despond alone; but he still struggled toward that side of the swamp which was furthest from his own house, and closest to the narrow-gate. But he could not get out, because of the heavy burden which was upon his back.

I then beheld in my dream, that a man came to him, whose name was Help, and asked him what he was doing there.

"Sir," Christian said, *"I was told to go this way by a man called Evangelist, who directed me to yonder narrow-gate, that I might escape the wrath to come. And as I was going, I fell into this swamp!"*

"But why did you not look for the steps?" asked Help.

"As I was hurrying along, I fell in!" replied Christian.

"Then," said Help, *"give me your hand!"*

So Christian reached out his hand, and Help drew him out of the mire, set him upon solid ground, and bid him to continue on his way.

Then Christian turned to Help and said, *"Sir, why is it, since the way from the City of Destruction, to yonder narrow-gate is over this swamp, that this bog is not mended, so that poor Pilgrims might travel there more safely?"*

Help then explained to Christian, *"This miry swamp is a place which cannot be mended. It is the pit where the scum and filth which attend conviction for sin, continually runs and therefore it is called the Swamp of Despond. For as the sinner is awakened about his lost condition, there arises in his soul many fears, and doubts, and discouragements, which all settle in this place. This is the reason why the swamp remains so foul.*

"It is not the pleasure of the King, that this place should remain so bad. His laborers have long been, by the directions of His Majesty, employed to mend this patch of ground. Yes, and to my knowledge, millions of wholesome instructions have, at all seasons, been brought from everywhere in the King's dominions, to help mend it. These are the best materials to make this place into solid ground, if it could have been mended. But it remains the Swamp of Despond still and so will it ever remain, even when they have done all that can be done.

"True, there are, by the direction of the Law-giver, certain good and

sturdy steps, placed through the very midst of this swamp. But at such times, this place spews out so much of its filth, that these steps are hardly seen. Or if they are seen, men may become dizzy, miss the steps and fall into the mire!"

Now I saw in my dream, that, by this time, Pliable had reached home, and his neighbors came to visit him. Some of them called him a wise man for coming back; and some called him a fool for attempting such a hazardous journey. Others mocked him for his cowardliness, saying, *"Surely, since you began the venture, you should not have been so weak as to have given up because of a few difficulties."*

So Pliable was ashamed, and began to sneak around among them. But eventually he gained more courage and his neighbors then began to ridicule him behind his back.

CHAPTER 4

MR. WORLDLY-WISEMAN

Now as Christian was walking by himself, he spotted someone afar off, traveling over the field and they happened to meet just as they were crossing each other's path. The gentleman's name was Mr. Worldly-wiseman. He dwelt in the town of Carnal Policy, a very large town, close by the City of Destruction, from whence Christian came. This man, meeting with Christian, had some knowledge of him, for Christian's leaving the City of Destruction was much talked about, not only where he had lived, but also it was the talk of the town in other places. Mr. Worldly-wiseman, therefore, beholding Christian's difficult journey, and observing his sighs and groans, and the like began to enter into conversation with Christian.

"Say there, friend, where are you going in this burdened manner?" asked Worldly-wiseman.

"A burdened manner, indeed, I think, as any poor creature ever had!" replied Christian. *"And since you ask me where I am going, I will tell you. Sir, I am going to yonder narrow-gate which is ahead of me. There, I am informed, I shall be instructed how to be rid of my heavy burden."*

"Have you a wife and children?" asked Worldly-wiseman.

"Yes," replied Christian *"but I am so weighed down with this burden on my back, that I cannot take pleasure in them as I once did. In fact, it is now as though I had no family at all."*

"If I give you counsel, will you take my advice?" asked Worldly-wiseman.

"If it is good counsel, I will," replied Christian, *"for I am in need of good advice."*

"I would advise you, then," responded Worldly-wiseman, *"that you rid yourself of that burden on your back, as quick as possible! For you can never have happiness or peace of mind until you do!"*

"That is what I am seeking for," answered Christian. *"I desperately want to be rid of this heavy burden, but I cannot get it off myself! Nor is there any man in our country who can remove it from my shoulders. Therefore I am going this way, as I told you, that I may be rid of my burden!"*

"Who told you that this was the way to rid you of your burden?" replied Worldly-wiseman.

"A man who appeared to be a very noble and honorable person," answered Christian. *"His name, as I remember, is Evangelist."*

"I curse him for that counsel!" snarled Worldly-wiseman. *"There is not a more dangerous and troublesome way in all the world! You shall find this out for yourself, if you follow his advice. I see that you have met with trouble already, for I see that the mire from the Swamp of Despond is upon you. That swamp is just the beginning of the sorrows which attend those who continue in that dangerous way.*

"Listen to me, for I am older than you. On that narrow way, you are sure to meet with weariness, pain, hunger, peril, sword, lions, dragons, darkness and what not! In a word, you will meet with death! These things are certainly true, having been confirmed by many testimonies. And why should you so carelessly cast yourself away, by giving heed to a stranger?"

"Why, Sir," answered Christian, *"this burden upon my back is more dreadful to me than all the things which you have mentioned! Indeed,*

I don't care what danger I meet with along the way, as long as I get deliverance from my burden!"

"How did you get your burden, in the first place?" questioned Worldly-wiseman.

"By reading this Book in my hand," answered Christian.

"I thought so!" snapped Worldly-wiseman, *"and it has happened unto you as to other weak men who, meddling with things too high for them, do suddenly fall into the same bewilderment that you now suffer. In this perplexing state, they undertake dangerous ventures, to obtain they know not what."*

"I know what I want to obtain," asserted Christian, *"ease from my heavy burden!"*

"But why do you seek for ease in this perilous way," asked Worldly-wiseman, *"seeing that so many dangers attend it? Especially since, had you but sense to listen to me, I could direct you how to obtain what you desire, without all these dangers! Yes, and with my remedy, you shall gain much safety, friendship, and happiness!"*

"Please, sir, reveal this secret to me!" begged Christian.

Worldly-wiseman began, *"Why, in yonder village named Morality, there dwells a gentleman whose name is Legality. He is a very sensible man, having a good reputation, who has ability to help remove such burdens like yours. Yes, to my knowledge, he has done a great deal of good this way and besides, he has skill to cure those who are somewhat crazed in their minds, because of their burdens. To him you may go, and be helped in a very short while. His house is not quite a mile from here; and if he should not be at home himself, his handsome young son, whose name is Civility, can help you as well as the old gentleman himself!*

"There, I say, you may be eased of your heavy burden; and if you do

*not want to return to the City of Destruction, and I encourage you not
to return, you may send for your wife and children to join you in this
village. In the town of Morality, there are many vacant houses one of
which you may have at a reasonable rate. It is inexpensive to live there
and all the neighbors are honest and fashionable. To be sure, this will
make your life more happy."*

Now Christian was somewhat in a dilemma; but he shortly concluded, that if what this gentleman had said was true, then his wisest course was to take the advice of Worldly-wiseman.

So Christian inquired, *"Sir, what is the way to this honest man's
house?"*

"Do you see yonder hill?" asked Worldly-wiseman.

"Yes, very well," replied Christian.

"You must go by that hill," directed Worldly-wiseman, *"and the first
house you come to, is his."*

So I saw in my dream, that Christian turned out of the narrow way,
to go to Mr. Legality's house for help. But, behold, when he got
near the hill, it was so high, and it so hung over him, that Christian was afraid to venture further, lest the hill should fall on his
head! Flashes of fire also came out of the hill, which made Christian
afraid that he should be burned alive!

Therefore he stood still and did not know what to do. His burden
now seemed even heavier to him, than when he was in the narrow
way. He was so frightened, that he trembled with fear! He now began to be very sorry that he had taken Worldly-wiseman's counsel.

Just then, he saw Evangelist coming to meet him, at whose sight, he
began to blush with shame. So Evangelist drew nearer and nearer;
and coming up to Christian, he gazed upon him with a solemn
countenance, and thus began to address Christian.

"What are you doing here, Christian?" asked Evangelist.

Christian did not know what to answer and stood speechless before him.

Then Evangelist continued, *"Are you not the man that I found weeping outside the City of Destruction?"*

"Yes, kind Sir, I am the man," replied Christian.

"Did I not direct you to the way which leads to yonder narrow-gate?" questioned Evangelist.

"Yes, dear Sir," Christian said.

"Why is it, then, that you have so quickly turned aside?" asked Evangelist, *"for you have now gone out of the narrow way!"*

Then Christian explained, *"Soon after I had gotten over the Swamp of Despond, I met a gentleman who persuaded me that in the village of Morality, I would find a man who could take off my burden."*

"What did this man look like?" asked Evangelist.

"He looked like a gentleman," replied Christian, *"and talked much to me, until he persuaded me to leave the narrow way. But when I saw this hill, and how it hung over the path, I could proceed no further, being afraid that it would tumble down on my head!"*

"What else did that gentleman say to you?" inquired Evangelist.

"Why, he asked me where I was going and I told him," responded Christian.

"And what did he say then?" asked Evangelist.

"He asked me if I had a family? And I told him yes, but I was so weighed down with the burden on my back, that I could not take pleasure in them as formerly," responded Christian.

"And what did he say then?" inquired Evangelist.

"He entreated me to get rid of my burden as fast as I could and I told him that this was the very thing I sought and that I was going to yonder gate, to receive further direction how I may get to the place of deliverance. Then he said that he would show me a better way, much shorter, which was not so attended with difficulties as the narrow way in which I was going. He said that this new way would bring me to a gentleman's house who had skill to take off my heavy burden. So I believed him, and turned out of the narrow way, hoping that I might soon be eased of my burden. But when I came to this place, and beheld these dreadful things, I stopped for fear of the danger and now I do not know what to do!"

"Then," said Evangelist, *"stand still a little, that I may show you the Words of God."*

So Christian stood trembling.

Then Evangelist began, *"See that you do not refuse to listen to the One who speaks from Heaven, 'The just shall live by faith, but if any man draws back, I will not be pleased with him.' Christian, you are the man who is running into this misery; you have begun to reject the counsel of the Most High God, and to draw back from the way of peace, even to the hazard of your soul's perdition!"*

Then Christian fell down at his feet as dead, crying, *"Woe is me, for I am undone!"*

At the sight of which, Evangelist caught him by the right hand, saying, *"All kinds of sin and blasphemies shall be forgiven. Stop doubting and believe."*

Then Christian began to revive, and stood up trembling before Evangelist.

Then Evangelist proceeded, saying, *"Give more earnest attention to the things I shall tell you. I will now show you who deluded you and to whom he sent you. The man whom you met is one named Mr. Worldly-wiseman, and he is rightly called; partly, because he delights in worldly thinking, and partly because he loves worldly teaching, for it saves him from the doctrine of the Cross of Christ. Therefore he always goes to the Town of Morality to church. And because he is of this worldly temper, he seeks to oppose the way of the Cross. Now there are three things in this man's counsel, that you must utterly abhor:*

First, his turning you out of the right way.

Secondly, his laboring to render the Cross odious to you.

Thirdly, his setting your feet in that way which leads unto eternal death.

"*First, You must abhor his turning you out of the right way and your consenting to his false guidance. This is to reject the counsel of God, for the sake of the counsel of the world. The Lord says, 'Make every effort to enter through the narrow-gate,' the gate to which I sent you. 'For narrow is the gate and straight is the way that leads to life, and only a few find it!' From this little narrow-gate, and from the narrow way, this wicked man has turned you, and has brought you almost to destruction! You must hate, therefore, his turning you out of the narrow way and abhor yourself for hearkening to him.*

"*Secondly, You must abhor his laboring to render the Cross odious unto you; for you are to prefer it 'before the treasures of Egypt!' Besides, Jesus, the King of glory has told you, that he who 'will save his life, shall lose it!' And, 'If anyone comes to Me and does not hate his father and mother, his wife and children, his brothers and sisters, yes, even his own life, he cannot be My disciple!' Therefore I say, if any man labors to persuade you that the Lord's counsel will lead to your death, you must completely abhor his false doctrine.*

"*Thirdly, You must hate his turning your feet into the way which leads unto death. And for this, you must consider to whom he sent you and also how unable that person is to deliver you from your heavy burden.*

"He to whom you were sent for relief, is Mr. Legality, the son of the Bondwoman who is in bondage to the Law, along with her children. She represents Mount Sinai, which is the mountain you feared would fall on your head. Now, if she, along with her children, are in bondage, how can you expect to be made free by them? This Mr. Legality, therefore, is not able to set you free from your burden. No one was ever freed from their burden by him. No, nor can this ever be, for you cannot be justified by the works of the Law; for by the deeds of the Law, no man can be rid of his burden! Therefore, Mr. Worldly-wiseman is a liar and Mr. Legality is a cheat! And as for his son Civility, notwithstanding his pleasant looks, he is but a hypocrite, and cannot help you either!

"Believe me, there is no substance in all this blustering talk which you have heard of these deceivers. Their only design is to cheat you out of your salvation, by turning you from the narrow way in which I had sent you."

After this, Evangelist called aloud to the heavens for confirmation of what he had said and immediately words and fire came out of the mountain under which poor Christian stood. This made the hair of his neck stand up.

These are the words that came forth: *"All who rely on observing the Law are under a curse, for it is written: Cursed is everyone who does not continue to obey all these commands that are written in the Book of the Law."*

Christian now expected nothing but death and began to cry out woefully. He even cursed the time when he met with Mr. Worldly-wiseman, calling himself a thousand fools for hearkening to his false counsel. He also was greatly ashamed to think that this man's worldly advice, coming only from human reasoning, should so easily prevail with him, as to cause him to forsake the right way.

Christian then spoke to Evangelist with great earnestness, *"Sir, is there any hope for me? May I now go back, and then proceed through the narrow-gate? Or shall I be abandoned in shame, because of my waywardness? I am sorry I hearkened to this man's false counsel. Can my sin ever be forgiven?"*

Then said Evangelist to him, *"Your sin is very great, for by it you have committed two evils: You have forsaken the right way, to tread in forbidden paths! Yet the man at the narrow-gate will still receive you. Only take heed that you never again turn aside, lest you perish in your disobedience, for God's anger can flare up in an instant!"*

Then Christian committed himself to return to the narrow way. Evangelist then kissed him, and encouraged him with a smile, commending him to God's safe keeping.

So Christian went on with haste, and did not speak to anyone along the way. And if anyone addressed him, he would not hearken to their counsel. He traveled like one who was treading on forbidden and dangerous ground, and could never feel himself safe, until he was back on the narrow way, which he had left to follow Mr. Worldly-wiseman's false advice.

CHAPTER 5

THE NARROW-GATE

So, in process of time, Christian arrived at the narrow-gate. Now, over the gate there was written, *"Knock, and it shall be opened unto you."*

He knocked, therefore, several times, saying, *"May I now enter here, though I have been an undeserving wretch? If so, I shall sing His everlasting praise!"*

At last, a serious person came to the gate, named Good-will, and asked who was there, from whence he came and what he wanted.

Christian responded, *"I am a poor burdened sinner, coming from the City of Destruction. I am going to the Celestial City, that I may be saved from the wrath to come. I have been informed Sir, that the way to the Celestial City is through this gate. Are you willing to let me enter?"*

Good-will replied, *"I am willing with all my heart!"* And with this, he opened the gate.

As Christian was stepping in, Good-will gave him a sudden yank.

Surprised, Christian asked, *"Why did you do that!"*

Good-will then explained, *"A short distance from this gate, there is a strong castle erected, of which Beelzebub is the prince. From there, both he and his minions shoot arrows at those who come up to this gate, hoping to kill them before they can enter in!"*

Then Christian said, *"I both rejoice and tremble!"*

When Christian was safely inside, the man at the narrow-gate asked him who had directed him there.

"Evangelist directed me to come here and knock, as I did," said Christian, *"and that you, Sir, would then tell me what I must do."*

"An open door is set before you and no man can shut it!" responded Good-will.

"I am now beginning to reap the benefits of my hazardous journey!" replied Christian.

"But how is it that you came alone?" asked Good-will.

"Because none of my neighbors saw their danger, as I saw mine," answered Christian.

"Did any of them know of your coming?" inquired Good-will.

Christian replied, *"Yes! My wife and children saw me at first, and called after me to come back. Also, some of my neighbors stood crying and calling for me to return; but I put my fingers in my ears and so I started on my journey."*

"But did none of them follow you, to attempt to persuade you to turn back?" asked Good-will.

"Yes!" replied Christian, *"both Obstinate and Pliable tried to turn me back; but when they saw that they could not prevail, Obstinate railed at me, and went back alone. But Pliable came with me for a little way."*

"But why did Pliable not come all the way here with you?" questioned Good-will.

Christian explained, *"Indeed, he did come with me, until we came to the Swamp of Despond, into which we suddenly fell! At that, Pliable became so discouraged, that he would not venture with me any further. Being thus disheartened, he got out of the swamp on the side nearest to his own house and he told me I could possess the heavenly country alone!*

So he went his way, following after Obstinate and I continued traveling to this narrow-gate."

Then Good-will said, *"Alas, poor Pliable! Is Celestial Glory of so small a value to him, that he does not count it worth running the hazard of a few difficulties to obtain it?"*

Christian then said, *"I have stated the truth concerning Pliable; but if I would also tell all the truth about myself, it would reveal that there is no difference between us! It is true that he went back to his own house, but I had also turned aside into the way of destruction, being persuaded by the worldly arguments of Mr. Worldly-wiseman."*

"Oh! That deceiver would have you seek ease from your burden at the hands of Mr. Legality! Both of them are liars and cheats! And did you take his counsel?" asked Good-will.

"Yes, as far as I dared!" confessed Christian, *"I went to find Mr. Legality, until I thought that the mountain on the way to his house would fall upon my head! So I was forced to stop!"*

"That mountain has been the death of many and will be the death of many more! It is fortunate that you escaped without being dashed to pieces!" exclaimed Good-will.

Christian answered, *"Truly, I do not know what would have become of me, had not Evangelist found me in my sad plight! But it was of God's mercy that he came to me, otherwise I would never have arrived at this narrow-gate. But now I am here safe, even I, who certainly am more fit to have died under that mountain, than to have arrived safely here. O! what a choice favor is this!"*

Good-will then said, *"We refuse entrance to no sincere Pilgrim, notwithstanding all the wickedness they have done before they arrive here. Therefore my friend, come with me, and I will teach you about the way in which you must go. Look ahead of you, do you see that narrow way?*

That is the way you must go. It was built by the patriarchs, prophets, Christ and His Apostles; and is as straight as can be. This is the only way you must go!"

"But," inquired Christian, *"Are there no turnings nor windings, by which a Pilgrim may lose his way?"*

"Yes, there are many side paths which intersect with the narrow way, but they are crooked and wide. This is how you may distinguish the right from the wrong, only the right path is straight and narrow!"

Then I saw in my dream, that Christian further asked if Good-will could help him remove the burden which was upon his back; for he could not remove it without help.

Good-will told him, *"Be content to bear your burden until you come to the place of deliverance; for there it will fall from your back all by itself."*

CHAPTER 6

THE HOUSE OF THE INTERPRETER

Then Christian began to prepare himself for his journey. Good-will told him that when he had traveled some distance from the Gate, he would come to the House of the Interpreter, and knocking at the door, he would be shown some valuable lessons. (Editor's note: Bunyan portrays the Interpreter, as an emblem of the Holy Spirit.)

Christian then said farewell to Good-will, who in turn bid him Godspeed. Christian traveled on until he came to the House of the Interpreter, where he knocked again and again. At last someone came to the door, and asked who was there.

"Sir," answered Christian, *"I am a traveler, who was told by a man named Good-will, to come here for help. Therefore I would like to speak with the master of this house."*

So the servant called for the master of the house, who shortly came, and asked Christian what he wanted.

"Sir," Christian explained, *"I have come from the City of Destruction, and am going to the Celestial City. I was told by Good-will, the man who stands at the narrow-gate, that if I came here, you would show me some lessons which would be a great help to me on my journey."*

"Come in!" invited Interpreter, *"And I will show you some profitable things."*

Interpreter commanded the servant to light a candle, and bid

Christian to follow them. So they proceeded to a private room, and opened the door. Inside the room, Christian saw a picture of a very serious man hanging on the wall. (Editor's note: Bunyan portrays the man in the portrait, as an emblem of a godly pastor.)

The man in the picture had his eyes lifted up to Heaven, the best of books in his hand, the law of truth written upon his lips, and the world behind his back! He stood as if he pleaded with men and a crown of gold hung over his head.

Then Christian said, *"What does this picture mean?"*

Interpreter explained, *"The man depicted in this picture is one in a thousand! He can beget children and nurse them himself when they are born! And as you see him with his eyes lifted up to Heaven, with the best of books in his hand, and the law of truth written on his lips, this is to show you that his work is to understand and unfold difficult things.*

"Similarly, just as you see him stand as if he pleaded with men, and also notice that the world is cast behind his back, and that a crown hangs over his head, this is to show you that he lightly values the things of the present world, because of his love and devotion to his Master's service. Such a one is sure to have eternal glory for his reward in the world to come.

"I show you this picture first, because the man whom it portrays is one who the Lord of the Celestial City provides to be your guide in the difficult situations that you may encounter along the way. Therefore pay attention to what I have shown you, lest, in your journey, you meet with some who pretend to lead you along the right path, while in reality their way leads to death!"

Then Interpreter took him by the hand, and led him into a very large parlor which was full of dust, because it was never swept. After Christian had contemplated this scene for a little while, the Interpreter called for a man to sweep the room. When he began to sweep, the dust began to so thickly swirl around the room, that Christian began to be choked by it!

Then Interpreter said to a maiden who stood nearby, *"Bring some water, and sprinkle the room!"* After she had done this, the parlor was then swept and cleansed with ease.

"What does this mean?" Christian inquired.

Interpreter explained, *"This parlor is the heart of a man which has never been sanctified by the sweet grace of the Gospel. The dust is his original sin and inward corruptions, which have defiled the whole man. He who began to sweep at first, is the Law. The maiden who brought and sprinkled the water, is the Gospel.*

"You saw that as soon as the man began to sweep, that the dust thickly swirled around the room, and became even more difficult to cleanse, nearly choking you to death. This is to show you that the Law, instead of cleansing the heart from sin, does in fact arouse sin, giving greater strength to it and causing it to flourish in the soul. The Law both manifests and forbids sin, but it has no power to subdue sin.

"Again, you saw the maiden sprinkle the room with water, upon which it was cleansed with ease. This is to show you, that when the Gospel comes in the sweet and precious influences thereof to the heart, then, I say, even as you saw the maiden subdue the dust by sprinkling the floor with water, just so is sin vanquished and subdued, and the soul made clean, through faith, and consequently fit for the King of glory to inhabit."

I saw, moreover, in my dream, that the Interpreter took Christian by the hand, and led him into a little room, where two little children sat, each one in his own chair. The name of the older one was Passion and the name of the younger one was Patience. Passion seemed to be much discontented, but Patience was very quiet.

Then Christian asked, *"What is the reason for Passion's discontent?"*

The Interpreter answered, *"The guardian would have them wait for their best things until the next year, but Passion wants everything now; while Patience is willing to wait."*

Then I saw that someone came to Passion, and brought him a bag of treasure, and poured it down at his feet, which he grabbed up and rejoiced in; and in doing so, he laughed Patience to scorn. But I saw that in a short while, that Passion had squandered everything away, and had nothing left to him, but rags.

Then Christian said to the Interpreter, *"Expound this matter more fully to me."*

Interpreter replied, *"These two lads are symbolic: Passion is a symbol of the people of this world; and Patience is a symbol of the people of the world which is to come. As you see here, Passion will have everything now, that is to say, in this life. Just so are the people of this world, they must have all their good things now, they cannot wait until next year, that is, until the next world, for their portion of good.*

"That proverb, 'A bird in the hand is worth two in the bush,' is of more authority with them, than are all the Scripture testimonies of the value of the world to come. But as you saw that Passion had quickly lavished everything away, and had nothing left but rags, so will it be with all such people at the end of this world."

Then Christian declared, *"Now I see that Patience showed the best wisdom and that upon many accounts. First, because he waits for the best things; and second, because he will have the enjoyment of his good things, when Passion has nothing but rags!"*

Interpreter replied, *"True, and you may add another reason, namely, the glory of the next world will never end; but these earthly enjoyments will be suddenly gone. Therefore Passion had no reason to laugh at Pa-*

tience, just because he had his good things first; as Patience will have to laugh at Passion, because he will have his best things last! He, therefore, who has his portion first, only has this present life to spend it; but he who has his portion last, will have it everlastingly. Therefore it is said of the rich man: You in your lifetime have received your good things, just as Lazarus has received bad things; but now he is comforted, and you are in agony!"

Christian stated, *"Then I perceive that it is not best to covet present earthly things, but rather to wait for things to come."*

Interpreter responded, *"You say the truth, for the things which are seen are temporal; but the things which are unseen are eternal!" This is so, because present things and our fleshly appetites, are such near neighbors to one another; and also because worldly thinking and things to come, are such strangers to one another."*

Then I saw in my dream, that the Interpreter took Christian by the hand, and led him into a place where a fire was burning against a wall. Someone was standing by the fire, continually throwing great amounts of water upon it, attempting to quench it; yet the fire burned higher and hotter.

Then Christian asked, *"What does this mean?"*

The Interpreter answered, *"This fire is the work of grace which is operating in the heart. The one who casts water upon it, desiring to extinguish and put it out, is the Devil. Now I will show you the reason why the fire burns higher and hotter, in spite of all the Devil's efforts."*

So the Interpreter took Christian around to the back side of the wall, where he saw a man with a jar of oil in His hand, which He continually but secretly, cast onto the fire.

Then Christian questioned, *"What does this mean?"*

The Interpreter answered, *"This is Christ, who continually, with the*

oil of His grace, maintains the work already begun in the heart. By
this means, notwithstanding all that the devil can do, the souls of His
people are graciously preserved. And in that you saw that the man stood
behind the wall to maintain the fire, that is to teach you that it is hard
for the tempted believer to see how this work of grace is maintained in
the soul."

I saw also, that the Interpreter took Christian again by the hand,
and led him into a pleasant place, where a stately palace was built,
which was beautiful to behold. At the sight of which, Christian was
greatly delighted. He saw upon the top of the palace, that certain
people were walking, who were clothed all in gold.

Then Christian inquired, *"May we go in there?"*

Then the Interpreter took him, and led him towards the door of the
palace. And behold, at the door stood a great company of men, just
as desirous to go in, but dared not. A short distance from the door,
sat a man with a book and a pen at a table, to write down the name of
any who would enter therein. Christian also saw that in the doorway,
many men in armor stood to guard the palace from intruders.

Christian was somewhat bewildered at this. At last, when every
man stood back for fear of the armed men, Christian saw a man
who looked very determined, come up to the man at the desk, saying, *"Write down my name, Sir!"*

When the man at the desk had finished writing, Christian saw the
man draw his sword, put a helmet on his head, and rush toward the
door to the armed men, who battled him with deadly force. But
the man, not at all discouraged, started cutting and hacking most
fiercely. So after he had received and given many wounds to those
who attempted to keep him out, he cut his way through them all,
and pressed forward into the palace.

Then there was a pleasant voice heard from those who were within the palace, saying, *"Come in, come in! Eternal glory you shall win!"*

So he went in, where he was clothed with the same garments as those inside. Then Christian smiled and said, *"I think I truly know the meaning of this."*

"Now," Christian said, *"let me continue on my journey."*

"Not just yet," said the Interpreter, *"until I have showed you a little more and after that you may go on your way."*

So he took him by the hand again, and led him into a very dark room, where a man in an iron cage sat. Now this man seemed very sad, he sat with his eyes looking down to the ground, his hands folded together, and he sighed as if his heart were breaking.

Christian asked, *"What does this mean?"*

The Interpreter then told Christian to inquire of the man himself.

So Christian asked the man, *"What are you?"*

The man answered, *"I am now, what I once was not."*

Christian responded, *"What were you once?"*

The man said, *"I was once a fair and flourishing professor, both in my own eyes, and also in the eyes of others! I once was, as I thought, headed for the Celestial City; and had joy at the thought that I would get there."*

Christian further questioned, *"Well, what are you now?"*

The man responded, *"I am now a man of despair, and am locked up in despair, as in this iron cage. I cannot get out. O, I cannot escape!"*

Christian then inquired, *"But how did you get into this miserable condition?"*

The man in the iron cage replied, *"I stopped watching and being serious. I let my worldly lusts reign. I sinned against the light of God's Word, and His goodness. I tempted the devil and he has come to me! I have provoked God to anger and He has left me! I have so hardened my heart, that I cannot repent!"*

Then Christian asked the Interpreter, *"Is there no hope for such a man as this?"*

Then the Interpreter said to the man in the iron cage, *"Is there no hope, must you always be kept in this iron cage of despair?"*

The man replied, *"No, there is no hope at all."*

Interpreter responded, *"Why should you have no hope? Jesus is full of mercy."*

The man in the iron cage answered, *"I have crucified Him afresh; I have scorned His person; I have despised His righteousness; I have counted His blood as an unholy thing; I have insulted and disdained the Spirit of grace. Therefore I have shut myself out of all the promises, and there now remains nothing for me but threatenings, dreadful threatenings, fearful threatenings of certain judgment and fiery indignation, which shall devour me as God's adversary!"*

Interpreter then asked, *"For what did you bring yourself into this dreadful condition?"*

The man responded, *"For the lusts, pleasures, and profits of this world, in the enjoyment of which, I promised myself much delight. But now, every one of those things bite me, and gnaw me like a burning worm!"*

Interpreter then questioned, *"But can't you now repent and turn back to God?"*

The man answered, *"God has denied repentance to me. His Word gives me no encouragement to believe. Yes, He Himself has shut me up in this iron cage! Not all the men in the world can free me. O eternity! eternity! How shall I grapple with the misery that I must meet with in eternity!"*

Then the Interpreter said to Christian, *"Let this man's misery be remembered by you and be an everlasting warning to you!"*

"Well," Christian said, *"this is most fearful! May God help me to always watch and to pray that I may shun the cause of this man's misery! Sir, is it now time for me to go on my way?"*

Interpreter replied, *"Wait until I show you one last thing and then you shall go on your way."*

So he took Christian by the hand again, and led him into a room, where there was a man rising out of bed; and as he put on his clothing, he shook and trembled.

Then Christian asked, *"Why does this man thus tremble?"*

The Interpreter then bid the man to tell Christian the reason of his trembling.

So the trembling man began, *"This night, as I slept, I dreamed and behold, the heavens grew exceedingly black; also it thundered and lightninged in a most frightening way, so that it put me into a fearful agony!*

"So I looked up in my dream, and saw the clouds driven violently by the wind, upon which I heard a loud blast of a trumpet, and also saw a Man sitting upon a cloud, attended with thousands of angelic beings, all in flaming fire! Also the heavens were in a burning flame! I then heard a voice command, 'Arise you who are dead and come to your judgment!' And with that, the rocks shattered, the graves opened and the dead came forth! Some of them were exceedingly glad, and looked upward, while others sought to hide themselves under the mountains!

"Then I saw that the Man who sat upon the cloud opened the book, and commanded all people to draw near. Yet there was, by reason of a fierce flame which issued out and came from before Him, a great distance between Him and them, as between the judge and the prisoners at the bar. Then the Man who sat on the cloud commanded the angelic beings, 'Gather the tares, the chaff, and stubble together and cast them into the burning lake of fire!' And with that, the bottomless pit opened,

just where I stood! Out of the mouth of the pit spewed forth great billows of smoke and coals of fire, along with hideous noises!

"The angelic beings were then commanded, 'Gather My wheat into the barn!' And with that, I saw many caught up and carried away into the clouds, but I was left behind! I then sought to hide myself, but I could not, for the Man who sat upon the cloud fixed His eye upon me! My sins then came to mind and my conscience accused me on every side! At this, I awakened from my sleep."

Christian then asked, *"What was it which made you so afraid of this sight?"*

The trembling man replied, *"Why, I thought that the day of judgment had come and that I was not ready for it! But what frighted me the most, was that the angels gathered up several people near me and left me behind! Then the pit of Hell opened its mouth just where I stood! My conscience, too, afflicted me! And, as I stood there, the Judge continually kept His eye upon me, with a look of angry disapproval on His face."*

Then the Interpreter said to Christian, *"Have you considered all these things?"*

"Yes," replied Christian, *"and they cause me to both hope and fear!"*

"Then," stated the Interpreter, *"keep all of these things in your mind, so that they may spur you forward in the way you must go."*

So Christian began to prepare himself to continue on his journey.

Then the Interpreter declared, *"May the Comforter always be with you, good Christian, to guide you in the way that leads to the Celestial City!"*

So Christian went on his way, saying *"I have seen rare and profitable things here! Pleasant things and dreadful things. May I think on them, and remember the lessons they taught me. I am thankful, O good Interpreter, to you."*

CHAPTER 7

THE CROSS

Now I saw in my dream, that the highway up which Christian was to go, was fenced on both sides with a wall, and that wall was called 'SALVATION'. Up this way, therefore, burdened Christian ran, but not without great difficulty, because of the heavy load on his back. He ran on thus until he came to a place where there was a hill, and upon that hill stood a Cross; and a little below, at the bottom, was a sepulcher.

So I saw in my dream, that just as Christian came up to the Cross, his burden fell off his shoulders and back, and began to tumble, until it came to the mouth of the sepulcher, where it fell in, and I saw it no more!

Then Christian was glad and joyful, and said with a merry heart, *"Jesus has given me rest by His sorrow, and life by His death!"*

So he stood still awhile to ponder and wonder; for it was very surprising to him, that the sight of the Cross should thus ease him of his burden. He looked, therefore, and looked again, until tears flowed down his cheeks!

Now, as he stood looking and weeping, behold, three Shining Ones came to him and greeted him with *"Peace unto you."*

The first said to him, *"Your sins are forgiven!"*

The second stripped him of his rags, and clothed him with fine new clothes.

The third Shining One put a mark on Christian's forehead, gave him a scroll with a seal upon it and encouraged him to read it on his journey. He told Christian that he should turn it in at the Celestial Gate. So the Shining Ones left Christian and went on their way.

Then Christian gave three leaps for joy, and went on singing:

"Thus far did I come laden with my sin;
Nor could anything ease the grief that I was in.
Until I came here, What a place is this!
This must be the beginning of my bliss!

"For here, the burden fell from off my back,
And here, the chains that bound it to me, did crack!
Blessed Cross! Blessed sepulcher! Blessed rather be,
The Man who there, was put to shame for me!"

CHAPTER 8

SIMPLE, SLOTH AND PRESUMPTION

Then I saw in my dream, that Christian went on thus, until he came to a valley, where he saw, a little out of the way, three men fast asleep, with fetters upon their legs. The name of the one was Simple, the next Sloth, and the third Presumption.

Then Christian seeing them fast asleep, went to them, if perhaps he might awaken them, and cried, *"You are like those who sleep on the top of a mast, for the Dead Sea is under you, a gulf which has no bottom! Wake up! Wake up and I will help you take off your fetters!"*

He also warned them, *"If he who prowls about like a roaring lion comes by, you will most certainly be devoured!"*

They then looked upon him, and Simple replied, *"I see no danger!"*

Sloth said, *"Yet a little more sleep!"*

And Presumption said, *"Every tub must stand upon its own bottom, so we don't need your help!"*

And so they lay down to sleep again and Christian continued on his way. Yet was he troubled to think that men in such danger should so little regard the kindness which he so freely offered, by awakening them, warning them, and offering to help to remove their fetters.

CHAPTER 9

FORMALIST AND HYPOCRISY

And as he was troubled about this, he spotted two men come tumbling over the wall on the left side of the narrow way. They soon caught up to Christian, and entered into conversation with him. The name of the one was Formalist, and the name of the other Hypocrisy.

Christian asked, *"Gentlemen, where have you come from and where are you going?"*

Formalist and Hypocrisy answered, *"We were born in the land of Vain-glory, and are going to the Celestial City for reward."*

Christian responded, *"Why did you not enter in at the gate which stands at the beginning of the way? Do you not know that it is written that the one who does not enter by the gate, but climbs up some other way, that person is a thief and a robber?"*

Formalist and Hypocrisy replied, *"To journey to the gate for entrance, was considered too far away by all our countrymen. Besides that, our custom is to always make a short-cut, and climb over the wall."*

Christian questioned, *"But will it not be counted a trespass against the Lord of the city where we are going, to thus violate His revealed will?"*

Formalist and Hypocrisy told Christian that he need not trouble his head about this. For they had a tradition for what they were doing; and, if need be, they could produce witnesses to it, showing that this has been done for more than a thousand years!

"But," Christian said, *"will your practice stand a trial at law?"*

They told him that their tradition, being more than a thousand years old, would doubtless be admitted as legal by any impartial judge.

"And besides," they said, *"if we get into the way, what does it matter how we got there? If we are in, we are in! You are in the way to the Celestial City and you came in at the gate. And we are in the same way and we came tumbling over the wall. So how is your condition any better than ours?"*

Christian explained, *"I walk by the rule of my Master; but you walk by the vain working of your imaginations. You are accounted as thieves already, by the Lord of the way! Therefore, you will not be found to be true Pilgrims at the end of the journey. You came in by your own way, without His direction; and you shall go out by yourselves, without His mercy!"*

To this, they made but little answer; they only told Christian to pay attention to himself.

Then I saw that they went on in their own ways, without much conversation with one another; except that the two men told Christian, that as to laws and ordinances, they had no doubt but that they were as careful to do them as he was. *"Therefore,"* said they, *"we do not see how you differ from us, except for that coat which is on your back, which probably was given to you by some of your neighbors, to hide the shame of your nakedness."*

Christian answered, *"You cannot be saved by laws and ordinances and you did not come in at the narrow-gate. And as for this coat which is on my back, it was given to me by the Lord of the place where I am going and just as you say, to cover my nakedness. I take this as a token of His kindness to me, for I had nothing but rags before! With this, I comfort myself as I go: Surely, when I come to the gate of the Celestial City, the*

Lord will recognize me, since I have His coat on my back, a coat which He gave me on the day when He stripped me of my rags.

"I have, moreover, a mark on my forehead, which perhaps you have not noticed, which one of my Lord's most intimate associates fixed there on the day that my burden fell off my shoulders! I tell you, furthermore, that I was then given a sealed scroll, to comfort me by reading it as I travel along the way. I was also told to turn it in at the Celestial Gate, as my authorization to enter. But you lack all of these things, since you did not enter in at the narrow-gate!"

To this, they gave him no answer. They only looked at each other and laughed.

Then I saw that they went on, and that Christian walked on ahead, no longer talking to Formalist and Hypocrisy. He would ponder to himself, sometimes sighing, and sometimes content. Also, he would be often reading in the scroll that one of the Shining Ones had given him, which gave him refreshment.

CHAPTER 10

THE HILL DIFFICULTY

I beheld, then, that they all went on until they came to the foot of
the Hill Difficulty, at the bottom of which was a spring. Here there
also were two other ways besides that path which came straight
from the narrow-gate, one turned to the left hand, and the other
to the right; however the narrow way went straight up the Hill
Difficulty.

Christian now went to the spring, and drank to refresh himself, and
then began to go up the hill, saying,

> *"The hill, though high, I choose to ascend,*
> *The difficulty will not me offend;*
> *For I perceive the way to life lies here.*
> *Come, take heart, let's neither faint nor fear;*
> *Better, though difficult, the right way to go,*
> *Than wrong, though easy, where the end is woe."*

The other two men also came to the foot of the hill. When they
saw that the hill was very steep and high, and that there were two
other easier ways to go; and supposing that these two ways might
meet again on the other side of the hill with the same hard way that
Christian chose; they resolved to go in those easy paths.

Now the name of one of those ways was Danger and the name of
the other Destruction. So one took the way called Danger, which
led him into an enormous bewildering forest and the other took

the way to Destruction, which led him into a wide field full of dark pits, where he stumbled and fell, and rose no more.

I then looked at Christian going up the hill, where, because of the steepness of the hill, I saw he went from running to walking, and from walking to crawling on his hands and knees. Now, about midway to the top of the hill was a pleasant arbor, made by the Lord of the hill for the refreshment of weary travelers. When Christian arrived there, he sat down to rest. He then pulled his scroll out of his bosom, and read to his comfort. He also began to examine the garment that was given him while at the Cross.

Thus refreshing himself for a while, he at last fell into a slumber, and thence into a sound sleep, which delayed him there until it was almost night. While asleep, his scroll fell out of his hand.

Now, as he was sleeping, one came and awakened him, saying, *"Go to the ant, you sluggard, consider her ways, and be wise!"*

With that, Christian suddenly jumped up, and hurried on his way until he came to the top of the hill.

CHAPTER 11

TIMOROUS AND MISTRUST

Now, when he reached the top of the hill, two men came running to meet him, the name of one was Timorous, and the other Mistrust.

Christian inquired of them, *"Sirs, what is the matter? You are running the wrong way!"*

Timorous answered, *"We were going to the Celestial City, but, the further we go, the more dangers we meet with! Therefore we have turned around, and are going back."*

"Yes," said Mistrust, *"for there were lions just ahead of us on the path and we did not know if they were asleep or awake. We were terrified that they would tear us to pieces!"*

Then Christian said, *"You frighten me, but where shall I flee to be safe? If I go back to my own country, which shall be destroyed by fire and brimstone, I will certainly perish there! I shall only be safe, if I can reach the Celestial City. I must venture onward. To go back is nothing but death, to go forward is fear of death, and everlasting life beyond it. Therefore, I must surely go forward."*

So Mistrust and Timorous ran down the hill, and Christian continued on the difficult way.

Thinking of what he heard from the men, he felt in his bosom for his scroll, that he might read from it and be comforted; but he could not find it. Christian was then in great distress, and did not know what to do, for the scroll was his pass into the Celestial City.

Therefore, he was fearful and bewildered, not knowing what to do. At last, he remembered that he had slept at the arbor on the side of the steep hill. Falling down upon his knees, he asked God's forgiveness for his foolish act, and then went back to look for his scroll. Who can sufficiently set forth the sorrow of Christian's heart as he went back! Sometimes he sighed, sometimes he wept, and often he rebuked himself for being so foolish as to fall asleep in that arbor which was only erected for a little refreshment for weary Pilgrims.

Thus he went back, carefully looking on this side, and on that side, all the way as he went, hoping perhaps that he might find his scroll which had been his comfort so many times on his journey.

So he went on until he again came within sight of the arbor where he had rested and slept. But that sight only increased his sorrow, by bringing his folly of sleeping once again into his mind. Thus he bemoaned, *"O what a wretched man I am, that I should sleep in the day time, and in the midst of difficulty, that I should so indulge my flesh! For the Lord of the hill has built this arbor only for the refreshment of Pilgrims!*

"How many steps have I taken in vain! Thus it happened to Israel, for their sin, they were sent back again by the way of the Red Sea. Just so, I am made to retrace those steps with sorrow, which I might have trod with delight, had it not been for my folly of sleeping. How much further along my way might I have been by this time, but I had to tread these steps three times, which I only needed to have trod but once. Yes, now I must journey in the dark of night, for the daylight is almost gone. O that I had not slept!"

Reaching the arbor, he sat down and wept. Then, looking around sorrowfully under the bench, he spotted his scroll! With trembling and haste, he snatched it up and put it into his bosom.

None can tell how joyful he then was, for this scroll was the assurance of his salvation and his pass to the Celestial City. Therefore he secured it in his bosom, gave thanks to God for directing his eye to the place where it had fallen and with joy and tears resumed his journey.

O, how carefully now did he go up the rest of the hill! Yet, before he reached the top, the sun had gone down and this made Christian again recall the folly of his sleeping in the arbor. Thus once more, he began to reprove himself, *"O you sinful sleep! Now I must journey on in the dark and hear the frightful noises of the night creatures!"*

Just then, he remembered the report that Mistrust and Timorous warned him of, how they were frightened with the sight of the lions. Then Christian thought to himself, *"These beasts roam in the night for their prey; and if I should encounter them in the dark, how could I overcome them? How could I escape from being torn to pieces?"*

Thus Christian went on his way. But while he was thus bemoaning his difficult situation, he lifted up his eyes and behold, there was a very stately palace directly ahead. The name of the palace was Beautiful.

CHAPTER 12

THE PALACE BEAUTIFUL

So I saw in my dream, that Christian made haste and went forward, that if possible he might get lodging at the palace. Now before he had gone far, he entered into a very narrow passage, which was a short distance from the porter's lodge. Looking very intently ahead of him as he went, he spotted two lions in the way.

"Now," thought he, *"I see the dangers that Mistrust and Timorous were driven back by!"* Then he was afraid, and thought that he might go back as they had done, for he feared that nothing but death was before him.

But the porter at the palace, whose name is Watchful, perceiving that Christian halted as if he would go back, cried out to him, saying, *"Is your strength so small? Do not fear the lions, for they are chained, and are placed there for a trial of faith, and for the discovery of those who are faithless. Keep in the midst of the path, and no harm shall come unto you."*

Then I saw that Christian went on, trembling for fear of the lions. Taking heed to the directions of the porter, he heard them roar, but they did no harm to him. Then he clapped his hands in joy, and went on until he came and stood before the gate where the porter was.

Then Christian asked the porter, *"Sir, what residence is this? May I lodge here tonight?"*

The porter answered, *"This palace was built by the Lord of the hill, and He built it for the relief and security of Pilgrims."*

The porter also asked whence he came, and where he was going.

CHRISTIAN: *"I have come from the City of Destruction, and am going to the Celestial City; but because the sun has now set, I desire, if I may, to lodge here tonight."*

PORTER: *"What is your name?"*

CHRISTIAN: *"My name is now Christian, but at first my name was Graceless."*

PORTER: *"But why have you come so late, since the sun has set?"*

CHRISTIAN: *"I would have been here sooner, but, wretched man that I am, I slept at the arbor on the hillside. Besides that, while I slept, I lost my scroll, and traveled without it to the top of the hill. Then feeling for it, and not finding it, I was forced, with sorrow of heart, to go back to the place where I had slept. There I found it, and hence I have arrived here so late."*

PORTER: *"I will call for one of the maidens of the palace, who, if she approves of you, according to the rules of the palace, will bring you in to the rest of the family."*

So Watchful rang the bell. At this sound a noble and beautiful maiden, named Discretion, came to the door and asked why she was summoned.

The porter answered, *"This man is on a journey from the City of Destruction to the Celestial City, but being weary from traveling all day, he asked me if he might lodge here tonight. So I told him I would call for you, who, after talking with him, may do what seems best to you, according to the law of the palace."*

Then she asked Christian where he came from, and where he was going and he told her. She also asked him how he got into the narrow way and he told her. Then she asked him what he had seen and met with along the way and he told her. And lastly, she asked his name.

So he answered, *"My name is Christian. I have a great desire to lodge here tonight, because, by what I perceive, this palace was built by the Lord of the hill, for the relief and safety of Pilgrims."*

So she smiled, but tears came to her eyes. After a little pause, she said, *"I will summon two or three more of the family."*

So she hastened to the door, and called for Prudence, Piety, and Charity, who, after a little more discussion with him, brought him in to the family. Many of them met him at the threshold of the palace, and said, *"Come in, O blessed of the Lord! This place was built by the Lord of the hill, to accommodate such Pilgrims as yourself."*

Then he bowed his head, and followed them into the palace. So when he had come in and sat down, they gave him something to drink, and agreed that for the best improvement of time, they would converse with Christian until supper was ready.

PIETY: *"Come, good Christian, tell us of everything that has happened to you on your pilgrimage."*

CHRISTIAN: *"Gladly, and I am thankful that you are lodging me."*

PIETY: *"What moved you to commence a Pilgrim's life at first?"*

CHRISTIAN: *"I was driven out of my native country by dreadful news; namely, that unavoidable destruction awaited me, if I remained in that place."*

PIETY: *"How did it happen that you came out of your country by this way?"*

CHRISTIAN: *"It was as God would have it; for when I was under fear of destruction, I did not know where to go. Then it happened that a man named Evangelist came to me while I was trembling and weeping. He showed me the way to the narrow-gate, which I would never have otherwise found. It was he who directed me into the way that has led me to this palace."*

PIETY: *"Did you come by the house of the Interpreter?"*

CHRISTIAN: *"Yes, and I saw such things there, that I will remember as long as I live! Especially these three things: How, in spite of Satan's schemes, Christ maintains His work of grace in the heart. Secondly, how a man had so sinned himself into despair that he had no hope of God's mercy. Thirdly, the dream of one who imagined that the day of judgment had come, and he was not prepared."*

PIETY: *"Did you hear him tell his dream?"*

CHRISTIAN: *"Yes, and a dreadful one it was! It made my heart ache as he was telling of it, but yet I am glad I heard it."*

PIETY: *"Was that all that you saw at the house of the Interpreter?"*

CHRISTIAN: *"No, he showed me a stately palace, and how the people who were in it were clad in gold; and how a courageous man came and cut his way through the armed men who stood in the door to keep him out. He was then bid to come in, and win eternal glory. Those things ravished my heart! I would have stayed at that good man's house a year, but I knew I had further to go on my journey."*

PIETY: *"And what else did you see along the way?"*

CHRISTIAN: *"See! Why, I went but a little further, and I saw One hanging and bleeding upon a cross! The very sight of Him made my burden fall off my back (for I had groaned under a very heavy burden). It was an astonishing thing to me, for I had never seen such a sight before. Yes, and while I stood looking up, for I could not stop looking, three Shining Ones came to me. One of them testified that my sins were forgiven. Another stripped off my rags, and gave me this embroidered coat which you see. The third one put the mark which you see, on my forehead, and gave me this sealed scroll."* And with that, he plucked it out of his bosom.

PIETY: *"And what more did you see?"*

CHRISTIAN: *"The things that I have told you already, were the best. Yet as I traveled on, I also saw three men, Simple, Sloth, and Presumption, asleep a little out of the way, with iron chains on their legs. But there was nothing I could do to awaken them!*

"I also saw Formalist and Hypocrisy come tumbling over the wall, to go, as they imagined, to the Celestial City. I warned them of their folly, but they would not believe me. So they were quickly lost.

"But above all, I found it hard work to get up this hill and just as hard to go by the roaring lions. And truly if it had not been for the good porter who stands at the gate, I might have turned back. But now, I thank God that I am here, and I thank you for receiving me."

Then Prudence asked him a few questions.

PRUDENCE: *"Do you ever think of the country from whence you came?"*

CHRISTIAN: *"Yes, but with much shame and detestation. Truly if I had been mindful of that country from whence I came, I might have had opportunity to have returned, but now I desire a better country, that is, a heavenly one."*

PRUDENCE: *"Are you still hindered by some of your old habits?"*

CHRISTIAN: *"Yes, but greatly against my will, especially my worldly thoughts, with which all my countrymen, as well as myself, were delighted. But now all those things are my grief; and might I have my desires, I would choose never to think of those things again. For I have the desire to do what is good, but I have no ability to carry it out."*

PRUDENCE: *"Do you find sometimes as if you had overcome those worldly thoughts, yet find them still your annoyance at other times?"*

CHRISTIAN: *"Yes, but that is but seldom, and then they are to me as golden hours!"*

PRUDENCE: *"Can you remember by what means you find these annoyances, at times, as if they were overcome?"*

CHRISTIAN: *"Yes, when I think of what I saw at the Cross, that will do it. And when I look upon my embroidered coat, that will do it. Also when I look into the scroll that I carry in my bosom, that will do it. And when my thoughts are aglow about where I am going, that will do it."*

PRUDENCE: *"And why are you so desirous to go to the Celestial City?"*

CHRISTIAN: *"Why, it is there that I hope to see Him alive, who once hung dead on the Cross! And there I hope to be rid of all these hindrances which so constantly annoy me. In that wonderful place, there is no death and I shall dwell with those whom I best desire. For, to tell you the truth, I love Him, because He is the one who eased me of my heavy burden. Besides I am weary of the evil within me. I would gladly be where I shall die no more, and with the company who continually cry: Holy, holy, holy is the Lord Almighty!"*

Then Charity said to Christian, *"Have you a family? Are you a married man?"*

CHRISTIAN: *"I have a wife and four small children."*

CHARITY: *"And why did you not bring them along with you?"*

Then Christian wept, and said, *"O how willingly I would have done it! But all of them were utterly averse to my going on pilgrimage."*

CHARITY: *"But you should have talked to them, and have endeavored to have shown them the danger of staying behind."*

CHRISTIAN: *"So I did! I also told them what God had shown to me of the coming destruction of our city, but I seemed to them as a madman, and they did not believe me."*

CHARITY: *"And did you pray that God would bless your warnings to them?"*

CHRISTIAN: *"Yes, and with much affection, for surely my wife and poor children are very dear to me."*

CHARITY: *"And did you tell them of your own sorrow, and fear of destruction?"*

CHRISTIAN: *"Yes, over, and over, and over! They also saw my fears in my countenance, in my tears, and in my trembling under the dread of the judgment which hung over our heads! But all this was not sufficient to prevail with them to come with me."*

CHARITY: *"But what reason did they give as to why they would not come?"*

CHRISTIAN: *"Why, my wife was afraid of losing this world and my children were given to the foolish delights of youth! So by one thing or another, I was forced to go on pilgrimage alone."*

CHARITY: *"Yes, but though you warned them, was the example of your life a hindrance to them from going with you?"*

CHRISTIAN: *"Indeed, I cannot commend my life, for I am conscious of my many failings. I know also, that by a hypocritical life, a man may soon nullify all of his helpful reasonings with others. Yet this I can say, I was very careful not to give them any just occasion of making them averse to going on pilgrimage. They would tell me that I was too precise, and that I denied myself many things for their sakes, in which they saw nothing wrong. Also, I think I may say, that if what they saw in me hindered them, it was my great caution in not wanting to sin against God or others."*

CHARITY: *"Indeed Cain hated his brother because his own works were evil, and his brother's works were righteous. If your wife and children have been offended with you for this, they thereby show themselves to be implacable and you have delivered your soul from their blood!"*

Now I saw in my dream, that they thus sat talking together until supper was ready. When they sat down to eat, the table was abundantly furnished like a feast. All the talk at the table was about the Lord of the hill, about what He had done, and why He did what He did, and also why He had built that Palace.

By what they said, Christian perceived that He had been a great warrior, and with great danger to Himself, had fought with and slain him who had the power of death. This made Christian love Him all the more.

For, as they said, He did it with a great loss of blood. But that which put grace and glory into all that He did, was that He did it out of pure love to His people. There were some of the household who said they had spoken with Him since He died on the Cross. They have attested that they heard it from His own lips, that He is such a lover of poor Pilgrims, that none like Him can be found in all the world.

As an instance of what they affirmed, they told how He had stripped Himself of His glory, that He might die for poor sinners. They also heard Him say that He would not dwell in the Celestial City alone. They added, moreover, that He had advanced many Pilgrims to be princes, though by nature they were born beggars and objects of wrath.

Thus they discoursed together until late at night. After they had committed themselves to their Lord for protection, they went to their rooms to rest. Pilgrim was given a large upper chamber, whose window opened toward the sun-rising, the name of the chamber was Peace. There he slept until break of day, and then he awoke and sang:

> *"Where am I now, is this the love and care*
> *Of Jesus for the men that Pilgrims are?*
> *Thus to provide, that I should be forgiven,*
> *And dwell already the next door to Heaven!"*

So, in the morning, they all got up; and after additional discourse, they told him that he should not depart until they had shown him the rarities of that place.

First, they brought him into the study, where they showed him records of the greatest antiquity, in which was the lineage of the Lord of the hill, that He was the Son of the Ancient of Days by eternal generation. Here also were more fully recorded, the acts which He had done, and the names of many hundreds that He had taken into His service and how He afterwards brought them into an imperishable inheritance in His Father's house.

Then they read to him some worthy acts that some of His servants had done, how they had conquered kingdoms, wrought righteousness, obtained promises, shut the mouths of lions, quenched raging fire, escaped the edge of the sword; whose weakness was turned to strength; and who became mighty in battle, putting whole armies to flight.

They then read in another part of the records of the Palace, where it was shown how willing their Lord was to receive into His favor any, even the worst, though they in time past had offered great contempt to His person and works.

Here Christian also viewed several histories of many additional famous things, both ancient and modern. He saw prophecies and predictions of things which will have their certain accomplishment, both to the dread and amazement of their Lord's enemies, and the comfort and solace of His Pilgrims.

The next day they took him into the armory, where they showed him all kinds of armor which their Lord had provided for Pilgrims. There were swords, shields, helmets, breastplates, all-prayer, and shoes that would not wear out. Here was enough armor to equip as many men for the service of their Lord, as there are stars in the Heaven.

They also showed him the weapons with which some of his servants had done wonderful things. They showed him Moses' rod; the hammer and nail which Jael slew Sisera with; the pitchers and trumpets with which Gideon put the armies of Midian to flight. Then they showed him the oxgoad with which Shamgar slew six hundred men. They showed him, also, the jaw-bone with which Samson did such mighty feats. They showed him, furthermore, the sling and stone which David slew Goliath with. They showed him, moreover, many excellent things, with which Christian was much delighted. After that, they went to their chambers to rest again.

Then I saw in my dream, that on the morrow, Christian got up to resume his journey, but the others wished for him to stay until the next day. They said that they will, if the day is clear, show him the Delectable Mountains, which would further add to his comfort, as they were nearer his desired haven. So he consented and stayed.

When the morning came, they took him up to the top of the palace, and told him to look south. So he did, and behold, at a great distance, he saw a most pleasant mountainous country, beautified with woods, vineyards, fruits of all sorts, flowers, along with springs and fountains, all very delectable to feast one's eyes.

Then he asked the name of the country. They said that it was Immanuel's Land, and it is common for all Pilgrims to go there. *"When you arrive,"* said they, *"you may see to the gate of the Celestial City, as the shepherds who live there will show you."*

Now, just before Christian was about to leave, they asked him to go again into the armory. When they arrived, they equipped him from head to foot with armor, lest, perhaps, he would meet with assaults along the way. He being, therefore, thus attired, walked out with his friends to the door, and there he asked the porter if he had seen any Pilgrims pass by.

The porter answered, *"Yes."*

CHRISTIAN: *"Did you know him?"*

PORTER: *"I asked his name, and he told me it was Faithful."*

CHRISTIAN: *"Oh, I know him! He is my townsman, my near neighbor, he comes from the place where I was born. How far do you think he may be ahead of me?"*

PORTER: *"By this time he is perhaps beyond the bottom of the hill."*

CHRISTIAN: *"Well, good Porter, may the Lord be with you, and increase your blessings, for the kindness that you have shown to me."*

Then Christian began to go forward, but Discretion, Piety, Charity and Prudence, desired to accompany him down to the bottom of the hill. So they went on together, reminiscing their former discourses, until they came to the start of the descent down the hill.

Then Christian said, *"As it was difficult coming up, so far as I can see, it is dangerous going down."*

"Yes," said Prudence, *"so it is, for it is a hard matter for a man to go down into the Valley of Humiliation, as you are about to do, and not stumble along the way. Therefore we have come to accompany you down the hill."*

So they began to go down, but very cautiously. Yet Christian still stumbled a time or two.

Then I saw in my dream that these good companions, when they arrived at the bottom of the hill, gave Christian a loaf of bread, a bottle of wine, and a cluster of raisins. He then went on his way.

CHAPTER 13

BATTLE WITH APOLLYON

But now, in this Valley of Humiliation, poor Christian was grievously challenged. He had gone but a little way, before he spotted a foul fiend coming over the field to contend with him, his name was Apollyon. Then Christian began to be afraid, and to deliberate whether to go back or to stand his ground. But he again reasoned that he had no armor for his back. He therefore thought that to turn his back to Apollyon might give the fiend the greater advantage to easily pierce him with his darts. Therefore Christian resolved to stand his ground, for he thought, *"Had I no more in my mind than the saving of my life, it would be the best way to stand."*

So he went on, and Apollyon met him. Now the monster was hideous to behold, he was clothed with scales like a fish, he had wings like a dragon, feet like a bear, out of his belly came fire and smoke, and his mouth was like the mouth of a lion! When he had come up to Christian, he looked upon him with an arrogant stare, and thus began to dispute with him.

APOLLYON: *"Where have you come from and where are you going?"*

CHRISTIAN: *"I have come from the City of Destruction, which is the place of all evil and am going to the Celestial City."*

APOLLYON: *"By this I perceive that you are one of my subjects, for all that country is mine, and I am the prince of it. How is it, then, that you have run away from your monarch? Were it not that I hope you would return to my service, I would strike you down with one blow, to the ground!"*

CHRISTIAN: *"I was born, indeed, in your dominions, but your service was hard, and your wages were such as a man could not live on, for the wages of sin is death!"*

APOLLYON: *"There is no prince who will thus lightly lose his subjects, nor will I lose you! But since you complain of your service and wages, be content to come back, and the best that our country can afford, I promise to give you."*

CHRISTIAN: *"But I have pledged myself to another, even to the King of princes, so how can I, with fairness, go back with you?"*

APOLLYON: *"You have gone from bad to worse! It is common for those who have professed themselves to be His servants, after a while to give Him the slip, and return again to me. If you do so also, then all shall be well for you."*

CHRISTIAN: *"I have sworn my allegiance to Him. How, then, can I go back, and not be hanged as a traitor?"*

APOLLYON: *"You did the same to me, and yet I am willing to overlook that, if now you will yet turn again and come back."*

CHRISTIAN: *"What I promised to you was from my youthful foolishness. Besides, the King under whose banner I now stand is able to absolve me, yes, and to pardon my former compliance with you. Besides, O destroying Apollyon, to speak the truth, I like His service, His wages, His servants, His government, His company, and His country, better than yours. Therefore, cease trying to persuade me further. I am His servant, and I will follow Him!"*

APOLLYON: *"Consider again, what you are likely to meet with along the way that you are now going. You know that, for the most part, His servants come to a wretched end, because they are transgressors against me and my ways. How many of them have been put to shameful deaths! And, besides, you count His service better than mine, but He never delivers any who serve Him out of my hands. But as for me, how many times, as all the world very well knows, have I delivered those who have faithfully served me from Him, either by power or fraud. Just so, I will deliver you."*

CHRISTIAN: *"His refraining to deliver His servants at present, is on purpose to test their love, whether they will cleave to Him to the end. You say that they will come to a wretched ending, but in fact, it is most glorious. As for present deliverance, they do not much expect it, for they patiently wait for their triumph and they shall have it when their King comes in His glory with all of His angels."*

APOLLYON: *"You have already been unfaithful in your service to Him, so why do you think that you will receive His wages?"*

CHRISTIAN: *"In what, O Apollyon, have I been unfaithful to Him?"*

APOLLYON: *"You were discouraged at first setting out, when you were almost choked in the Swamp of Despond! You attempted wrong ways to be rid of your burden, whereas you should have waited until your King had taken it off! You sinfully slept and lost your scroll! At the sight of the lions, you were almost persuaded to go back! And when you talked of your journey, and of what you have heard and seen, you were secretly proud of all that you said and did!"*

CHRISTIAN: *"All this is true, and much more which you have left out! But the King whom I serve and honor, is merciful, and ready to forgive. Besides, I acquired these infirmities in your country and I have groaned under them, been sorry for them, and have obtained pardon from my King."*

Then Apollyon broke out into a furious rage, saying, *"I am an enemy to this King! I hate His person, His laws, and His people! I have come out on purpose to destroy you!"*

CHRISTIAN: *"Apollyon, beware what you do! I am on the King's highway, the way of holiness, therefore take heed!"*

Then Apollyon straddled over the whole road, and said, *"I am not afraid. Prepare yourself to die! I swear by my infernal den, that you shall go no further. Here I will spill your blood!"*

And with that, Apollyon threw a flaming dart at his heart, but Christian had a shield in his hand, with which he caught the dart, and so prevented that danger.

Then Christian prepared himself for battle, as Apollyon rushed at him, throwing darts as thick as hail! Yet notwithstanding all that Christian could do to avoid it, Apollyon wounded him in his head, his hand, and his foot, this made Christian slightly retreat.

Apollyon, therefore, continued his furious attack. Christian again took courage, and resisted as manfully as he could. This intense combat lasted for more than half a day, until Christian was nearly exhausted. For Christian, because of his wounds, was becoming weaker and weaker.

Then Apollyon, seeing his opportunity, forced himself closer to Christian, and wrestling with him, gave him a dreadful fall and with that, Christian's sword flew out of his hand. Then Apollyon almost pressed him to death, so that Christian began to despair of life.

Then Apollyon exclaimed, *"I am sure of you now!"*

But as God would have it, while Apollyon was fetching his last blow to make a full end of him, Christian nimbly stretched out his hand for his sword, and grasped it, saying, *"Do not gloat over me, O my enemy! Though I have fallen, I will again rise!"* And with that, he gave Apollyon a deadly thrust, which made him fall back, as one who had received a mortal wound.

Christian perceiving that, rushed at him, saying, *"In all these things we are more than conquerors, through Him who loved us!"*

And with that, Apollyon spread his dragon wings, and sped away, so that Christian saw him no more for a season.

No man can imagine what yelling and hideous roaring Apollyon made during all this combat and on the other side, what sighs and groans burst from Christian's heart. He struggled fiercely, until he perceived that he had wounded Apollyon with his two-edged sword. Then, indeed, he looked upward with thanksgiving.

So when the battle was over, Christian said, *"I will here give thanks to Him who delivered me out of the mouth of the lion, to Him who helped me against Apollyon."*

Then a hand came to him, with some of the leaves of the Tree of Life, which Christian took, and applied to the wounds which he had received in the battle, and was healed immediately. He also sat down to eat the bread, and to drink from the bottle which were given to him at the Palace Beautiful.

So being refreshed, Christian continued his journey, with his sword drawn in his hand; for he thought, *"I do not know but that some other enemy may be nearby."* But he met with no other attack from Apollyon through the remainder of the valley.

CHAPTER 14

THE VALLEY OF THE SHADOW OF DEATH

Now, at the end of the Valley of Humiliation, was The Valley of the Shadow of Death. Christian needed to go through it, because it was the only way to the Celestial City. Now this valley was a very solitary place. The prophet Jeremiah thus describes it: *"A wilderness, a land of deserts, and of pits, a land of drought, and of the shadow of death, a land that no man"* (but a Christian) *"passed through, and where no man dwelt."*

Now here Christian had a more difficult battle than in his fight with Apollyon, as you shall see by what follows.

I saw then in my dream, when Christian came to the borders of the Valley of the Shadow of Death, that two men, hurrying back, met him. They were children of those who brought back an evil report of the good land of Canaan. Christian then questioned as follows:

CHRISTIAN: *"Where are you going?"*

They cried, *"Back! back! And if you prize either peace or life, then you will turn back also!"*

"Why? what is the matter?" Christian wondered.

"Matter!" they exclaimed. *"We were going the same way as you are now traveling, and went as far as we dared. Indeed we were almost past being able to come back; for had we gone a little further, we would not have been here to bring the news to you."*

CHRISTIAN: *"But what have you met with?"*

MEN: *"Why, we were almost in the Valley of the Shadow of Death; but fortunately, we looked ahead, and saw the danger before we came to it!"*

CHRISTIAN: *"But what did you see?"*

MEN: *"See! Why, the valley itself, which is as dark as pitch. We saw hobgoblins, satyrs, and dragons of the pit. We also heard a continual howling and yelling, like people under unutterable misery, who sat bound in affliction and chains. And over that Valley hangs the discouraging clouds of confusion. Death always spreads his wings over it. In a word, it is in every way dreadful, and utterly chaotic!"*

CHRISTIAN: *"In spite of what you have said, yet this is the way to my desired haven."*

MEN: *"Though it is your way, we will certainly not choose it for ours."*

So they parted, and Christian went on his way, keeping his sword drawn in his hand, for fear that he should be assaulted.

I then saw in my dream, that as far as this valley stretched, there was a very deep ditch on the right hand. That is the ditch into which the blind have led the blind in all ages, and have both miserably perished there.

Behold, on the left hand was a very dangerous quagmire, into which, if even a godly man falls, he can find no bottom for his foot to stand on. Into that quagmire King David once fell, and no doubt would have been smothered, had not He who is able, plucked him out.

The pathway through this valley was exceedingly narrow, therefore Christian had great difficulty. For when he sought, in the dark, to shun the ditch on the one hand, he was ready to tip over into the mire on the other side! As he carefully sought to escape the mire, he would almost fall into the ditch! Thus he went on, sighing bitterly.

For besides the dangers mentioned above, the pathway was so dark, that often, when he lifted his foot to step forward, he did not know where, or upon what he would set it next.

About the midst of this valley, he saw the mouth of Hell, which was very close to the narrow path.

"Now," thought Christian, *"what shall I do?"*

The flame and smoke would continually come out in such abundance, with sparks and hideous noises, things which Christian could not fight with his sword, as he did Apollyon before.

Therefore he was forced to put his sword away, and take up another weapon, called All-prayer. So he cried out, *"O Lord, I beseech You, deliver my soul!"*

Thus he went on for a great while, with the flames still reaching towards him. He also heard doleful voices, and rushings to and fro, so that sometimes he thought he would be torn in pieces, or trodden down like mire in the streets! This frightful sight was seen, and these dreadful noises were heard by him for several miles.

Arriving at a place where he thought that he heard a company of fiends coming forward to meet him, he stopped and pondered what was best for him to do. Sometimes he had half a mind to go back, then again, he thought he might be already half way through the valley. He also remembered how he had already vanquished many dangers and that the danger of going back might now be much more, than for him to go forward. So he resolved to persevere on the dangerous path.

Yet the fiends came nearer and nearer and when they were almost upon him, he cried out with a most forceful voice, *"I will walk in the strength of the Lord my God!"* With this the fiends retreated, and came no further.

It is important to note, that now poor Christian was so bewildered that he did not know his own voice. Just when he had come near the mouth of the burning pit, one of the wicked ones snuck up stealthily behind him whispering and suggesting many grievous blasphemies to him, which he thought had proceeded from his own mind. This tried Christian more than anything that he met with before, to think that he would now blaspheme Him whom he loved so much! Yet, if he could have helped it, he would not have done it; but he had not the discretion either to stop his ears, or to know from whence these blasphemies came.

When Christian had traveled in this disconsolate condition for a considerable time, he thought that he heard the voice of a man somewhere ahead of him, saying, *"Though I walk through the valley of the shadow of death, I will fear no evil; for You are with me."*

Then he was glad, and for these reasons:

First, because he realized by this, that someone who feared God was in this valley, as well as himself.

Secondly, he realized that God was with him, in that dark and dismal state, though he could not perceive Him.

Thirdly, he hoped that he could overtake the person ahead of him, and to have company soon.

So Christian went on, and called to the person ahead of him. But that person did not know what to answer, for he also thought that he was alone.

By and by the day broke. Then Christian said, *"He has turned the shadow of death into the morning."*

Morning having come, Christian looked back, not out of a desire to return, but to see, by the light of the day, what hazards he had gone through in the dark. So he saw more perfectly the ditch which was on the one hand, and the quagmire which was on the other side. He also realized how narrow the way was, which lay between them both.

Now he saw the hobgoblins, satyrs, and dragons of the pit, but all were afar off, for during the day, they did not come near. Yet they were revealed to him, according to that which is written, *"He reveals the deep things of darkness and brings deep shadows into the light."*

Now Christian was much affected with his deliverance from all the dangers of his solitary way. These dangers, though he feared them more before, yet he saw them more clearly now, because the light of the day made them conspicuous to him.

Walking now in the daylight was another mercy to Christian; for though the first part of the Valley of the Shadow of Death was dangerous, yet this second part which he had yet to travel, was, if possible, far more dangerous.

From the place where he now stood, even to the end of the valley, the whole way was so full of snares, traps, snags, nets, pitfalls and entanglements, that had it now been dark, as it was when he traveled the first part of the valley, though he had a thousand lives, he still would have perished!

But just now the sun was rising. Then Christian said, *"His candle shines upon my head, and by His light I walk through darkness."*

In this light, therefore, he came to the end of the valley.

Now I saw in my dream, that at the end of this valley lay blood, bones, ashes, and mangled bodies of men, even of Pilgrims who had previously gone this way. While I was pondering this, I spotted a cave a little ahead of Pilgrim, where two giants, Pope and Pagan, dwelt in olden times. By their power and tyranny, the men whose bones, blood, ashes, and mangled bodies which lay there, had been cruelly put to death.

But Christian went by this place without much danger, whereupon I was somewhat bewildered. I have learned since, that Pagan has been dead for a long time.

As for Pope, though he is still alive, he is, by reason of old age, and also of the many defeats which he met with in his younger days, has grown so deranged in mind, and stiff in his joints, that he can now do little more than sit in his cave's mouth, glaring at Pilgrims as they go by, and biting his nails because he cannot get at them.

So I saw that Christian went on his way. At the sight of the old man who sat in the mouth of the cave, he could not tell what to think, especially because Pope spoke to him, though he could not go after Christian, saying, *"You will never mend, until more of you are burned!"*

But Christian was silent, and so went by without being harmed.

Then Christian sang:

> *"O world of wonders, I can say no less!*
> *That I should be preserved in that distress*
> *That I have met with here! O blessed be,*
> *That hand that from it has delivered me!*
> *Dangers in darkness, devils, Hell, and sin,*
> *Did compass me, while I this valley was in.*
> *Yes, snares and pits, and traps, and nets, did lie,*
> *My path about, that worthless, foolish I,*
> *Might've been caught, entangled and cast down,*
> *But since I live, let Jesus wear the crown!"*

CHAPTER 15

CHRISTIAN MEETS
WITH FAITHFUL

Now, as Christian went on his way, he came to a little ascent, which was built on purpose, that Pilgrims might see ahead of them. Therefore, Christian went up and looking forward, he saw Faithful ahead of him, on his journey.

Then Christian cried aloud, *"Ho! Ho! Wait for me, and I will be your companion."*

At that, Faithful looked behind him and Christian called again, *"Stop, wait until I catch up to you!"*

But Faithful answered, *"No, I am running for my life, for the Avenger of Blood is behind me!"*

At this, Christian roused, and putting forth all his strength, quickly caught up with Faithful, and even ran past him, so the last became the first. Then Christian smugly smiled, because he had gotten ahead of Faithful, but, not watching where he was going, he suddenly stumbled and fell, and was unable to get back up, until Faithful came to help him.

Then I saw in my dream, that they went on very amiably together, and had sweet conversation about the things that had happened to each of them on their pilgrimage.

CHRISTIAN: *"My honored and well-beloved brother, I am glad that*

I have caught up with you; and that God has made us so like-minded, that we can walk as companions in this very pleasant path."

FAITHFUL: *"I had thought, dear friend, to have had your company much sooner; for you started out before me, therefore I was forced to come alone thus far."*

CHRISTIAN: *"How long did you stay in the City of Destruction, before you set out on your pilgrimage?"*

FAITHFUL: *"Until I could stay no longer; for right after you left, there was great talk that our city would soon be burned down to the ground with fire from Heaven!"*

CHRISTIAN: *"What! Did our neighbors really talk so?"*

FAITHFUL: *"Yes, for a while it was the talk of the town!"*

CHRISTIAN: *"Were you the only one who fled to escape the danger?"*

FAITHFUL: *"Though there was, as I said, great talk about the eminent destruction of our city, yet I do not think they truly believed it. For in the heat of the discussions, I heard some of them deridingly speak of you, and of your desperate journey, for so they called your pilgrimage. But I did believe, and still do, that our city will be destroyed with fire and brimstone from above and therefore I have made my escape!"*

CHRISTIAN: *"Did you hear any talk of neighbor Pliable?"*

FAITHFUL: *"Yes, I heard that he followed you until he came to the Swamp of Despond, where, as some said, he fell in. Yet he would never admit to having done so, but I am sure he was bedabbled with the mire from the swamp."*

CHRISTIAN: *"And what did the neighbors say about him?"*

FAITHFUL: *"Since his coming back to the city, he has been harshly derided by all sorts of people! Some mock and despise him and scarcely* will any employ him. He is now seven times worse off than if he had never left the city!"

CHRISTIAN: *"But why should they be so much against him, since they despise the narrow way that he forsook?"*

FAITHFUL: *"O! they say, 'Hang him, he is a turn-coat! He is not true to his profession of religion!' I think that God has even stirred up his enemies to hiss at him, and make him a proverb, because he has forsaken the narrow way!"*

CHRISTIAN: *"Were you able to talk with him before you left the City of Destruction?"*

FAITHFUL: *"I did meet him once in the streets, but he slunk away on the other side, as one ashamed of what he had done. So I was unable to speak with him."*

CHRISTIAN: *"Well, at my first setting out, I had hope for Pliable, but now I fear he will perish in the overthrow of the city. For it has happened to him according to the true proverb: 'A dog returns to his vomit; and a sow, having been washed, to her wallowing in the mire!'"*

FAITHFUL: *"These are my fears for him too, but who can prevent his downfall?"*

CHRISTIAN: *"Well, neighbor Faithful, let us now talk of things which more immediately concern ourselves. So tell me what you have met with as you traveled along the way."*

FAITHFUL: *"I escaped the Swamp which you fell into, and got up to the gate without that danger, but I met with one named Wanton, who would have liked to have done great harm to me."*

CHRISTIAN: *"It was well that you escaped her net. Joseph also was greatly tempted by her, and he escaped her just as you did; but it nearly cost him his life. What did she do to you?"*

FAITHFUL: *"You cannot imagine what a flattering tongue she had! She strongly urged me to go with her, promising me all kinds of fleshly delights."*

CHRISTIAN: *"But did she promise you the contentment of a good conscience?"*

FAITHFUL: *"No, only the delights of the flesh."*

CHRISTIAN: *"Thank God that you have escaped her! The mouth of an adulteress is a deep pit, he who is abhorred by the Lord will fall into it!"*

FAITHFUL: *"I do not know whether I wholly escaped her or not."*

CHRISTIAN: *"Why, I trust that you did not consent to her evil desires?"*

FAITHFUL: *"No, not to defile myself; for I remembered an old writing which said, 'Her steps lead to Hell!' So I shut my eyes, that I would not be bewitched with her seductive looks. Then she maligned me, at which I quickly left her!"*

CHRISTIAN: *"Did you meet with any other assaults as you journeyed?"*

FAITHFUL: *"When I came to the foot of the Hill of Difficulty, I met with a very aged man, who asked me who I was and where I was going. I told him that I am a Pilgrim going to the Celestial City. Then the old man said, 'You look like an honest fellow, will you be content to dwell with me for the wages that I shall give you?' I asked him his name, and where he lived. He said his name was Adam the First, and that he dwelt in the town of Deceit.*

"I further asked him what his work was, and what were the wages that he would pay. He told me that his work was many delights; and his wages were that I should be his heir at last. He told me that his house was filled with all the dainties of the world. Then I asked if he had any children. He said that he had three daughters, the Lust of the Flesh, the Lust of the Eyes, and the Pride of Life, and that I could marry them all

if I desired. Then I asked how long he would have me to live with him. And he told me, as long as he lived himself."

CHRISTIAN: *"Well, what conclusion did you and the old man come to at last?"*

FAITHFUL: *"Why, at first, I found myself somewhat inclined to go with the man, for his words were very appealing to me. But as I talked with him, I saw written on his forehead, 'Put off the old man with his wicked deeds!'"*

CHRISTIAN: *"And what then?"*

FAITHFUL: *"Then it flashed into my mind, that whatever he said, and however he flattered me, that if he brought me to his house, he would sell me for a slave! So I told him to be quiet, for I would not come near the door of his house. Then he reviled me, and told me that he would send one after me, who would make my way most bitter! So just as I turned to leave him, I felt him take hold of my flesh, and he pulled me with such a fierce wrench, that I thought he had torn part of me off. This made me cry out, 'O what a wretched man I am!' So I escaped, and went on my way up the hill."*

"Now when I had gone about half way up, I looked behind me, and saw one coming after me, as swift as the wind. He overtook me just about the place where the arbor stands."

CHRISTIAN: *"That was the same place where I sat down to rest; and being overcome with sleep, I lost my scroll!"*

FAITHFUL: *"But, good brother, hear me out. As soon as the man overtook me, he gave me a blow, and knocked me down, nearly killing me. When I somewhat revived, I asked him why he abused me so. He replied, 'Because of your secret inclining to Adam the First!'*

"With that he struck me another deadly blow on my chest, and beat me down backward, so I lay at his feet as dead. When I recovered again, I

cried to him for mercy, but he said, 'I do not know how to show mercy!' And with that he knocked me down again. No doubt he would have made an end of me, but that One came by, and commanded him to refrain."

CHRISTIAN: "Who was it that made him stop?"

FAITHFUL: "I did not know Him at first, but as He went by, I noticed the holes in His hands, and in His side, then I concluded that He was our Lord. So I continued up the hill."

CHRISTIAN: "That man who overtook you was Moses. He spares none, neither does he know how to show mercy to those who transgress his law."

FAITHFUL: "I know it very well, for it was not the first time that he has met with me. It was he who came to me when I dwelt securely at home, and who told me that he would burn my house down over my head, if I stayed there."

CHRISTIAN: "But did you not see the Palace which stood there on the top of the hill?"

FAITHFUL: "Yes, and the lions too! But for the lions, I think they were asleep, for it was about noon. Because I had so much of the day before me, I passed by the porter, and continued down the hill."

CHRISTIAN: "He told me indeed, that he saw you go by, but I wish you had called at the house, for they would have shown you so many rarities, that you would have never forgotten them to the day of your death. But please tell me, did you meet anyone in the Valley of Humiliation?"

FAITHFUL: "Yes, I met with one named Discontent, who attempted to persuade me to go back with him. His reason was, that the valley was entirely without honor. He told me, moreover, that to go there would displease all my relatives, such as Pride, Arrogance, Self-conceit,

Worldly-glory, along with others, whom, he said, would be very much offended if I made such a fool of myself as to travel through the Valley of Humiliation."

CHRISTIAN: *"Well, and how did you answer him?"*

FAITHFUL: *"I told him that although all these whom he named might claim friendship with me, rightly so, for indeed they were my relatives according to the flesh, yet since I became a Pilgrim, they have disowned me, as I also have rejected them. Therefore they were now to me no more than if they had never been my kinsmen.*

"I told him, moreover, that he had misrepresented this valley, for humility comes before honor. I told Discontent that I would rather go through this valley to obtain the honor so highly valued by the wise, than to choose that which he esteemed more worthy."

CHRISTIAN: *"Did you meet with anything else in that valley?"*

FAITHFUL: *"Yes, I met with Shame; but of all the men that I met with in my pilgrimage, I think that he bore the wrong name. He would have been more appropriately named Shameless."*

CHRISTIAN: *"Why, what did he say to you?"*

FAITHFUL: *"What! Why, he objected against religion itself! He said that it was a pitiful, inferior, unmanly business for one to mind religion. He said that a tender conscience was an unmanly thing and that for a man to watch over his words and ways, which the most popular people use, would make him the ridicule of the times. He also said that only a few of the mighty, rich, or wise, were ever of my opinion and that these few were fools to venture the loss of all, for who knows what!*

"He also objected to the poor and despised condition of all the Pilgrims of the past, along with their ignorance, and lack of understanding of all the new scientific theories.

"Yes, he also berated me about a great many more things than I relate

here. He told me that it was a shame to sit convicted and mourning under a sermon, or to be deeply concerned about eternal realities. He also said that it was a shame to ask my neighbor to forgive my petty faults, or to make restitution where I had stolen from any.

"He also said that religion made a man appear odd and strange to the great people of this world and that Pilgrims were, for the most part, poor and lowly. To him, this was a great shame."

CHRISTIAN: "And what did you say to him?"

FAITHFUL: "Say! I was so ashamed and humiliated that I could not say anything at first. But at last, I began to consider, that 'What is highly valued among men, is detestable in God's sight!' Shame had told me what is acceptable by worldly men, but he told me nothing about what God desires and commands.

"I also thought that at the final judgment, we shall not be designated to death or life, according to the standards of the world, but according to the wisdom and law of the most High God. Therefore, what God says is indeed the best, though all men in the world may disagree with Him.

"Seeing, then, that God prefers His divine religion, and a tender conscience; and that those who make themselves fools for the kingdom of Heaven are the wisest; and that the poor man who loves Christ is richer than the greatest man in the world who hates Him, depart Shame, for you are an enemy to my salvation! Shall I take your side, against my sovereign Lord? If I am now ashamed of His ways and servants, how then shall I look Him in the face, and receive His blessing at His coming?

"Indeed, this Shame was a bold villain! I could scarcely shake him off. Yes, he continued haunting me and whispering in my ear, some of the hindrances which attend true religion. But at last I told him that it was in vain to attempt to further dissuade me. For those things which he so disdained, were the most glorious in my eyes. So at last I got past *this most troublesome person. When I had finally shaken him off, then I began to sing:*

> *The trials that those men do meet withal,*
> *Who are obedient to the heavenly call,*
> *Are manifold, and suited to the flesh,*
> *And come, and come, and come again afresh;*
> *That now, or sometime else, we by them may*
> *Be taken, overcome, and cast away.*
> *O let the Pilgrims, let the Pilgrims, then,*
> *Be vigilant, and act courageous like men."*

CHRISTIAN: *"I am glad, my brother, that you withstood this villain so bravely; for as you say, I think he has the wrong name. For he is so bold as to follow us in the streets, and to attempt to put us to shame before all men. He seeks to make us ashamed of that which is good. If he were not so audacious, he would never attempt to do as he does. But let us still resist him, for notwithstanding all his bravadoes, he is nothing but a brazen fool. 'The wise shall inherit honor,' said Solomon, 'but He holds fools up to shame!'"*

FAITHFUL: *"I think we must cry to Him for help against Shame. He would have us to be valiant for the truth upon the earth."*

CHRISTIAN: *"That is true. Did you meet anybody else in the Valley of Humiliation?"*

FAITHFUL: *"No, not I, for I had sunshine all the rest of the way through and also through the Valley of the Shadow of Death."*

CHRISTIAN: *"It was well for you, but it fared far otherwise with me. Almost as soon as I entered into the Valley of Humiliation, I had a long and dreadful combat with that foul fiend Apollyon! Yes, I truly thought he would have killed me, especially when he got me down and pressed me under him, as if he would have crushed me to pieces. Then he threw* me, and my sword flew out of my hand. He railed that he was sure of me now. But I cried to God, and He heard me, and delivered me out of all my troubles.

"Then I entered into the Valley of the Shadow of Death, and had no light for almost half the way through it. I thought I would have been killed there, over and over, but at last the day broke, and the sun arose, and I went through the remainder of this Valley with far more ease and quiet."

CHAPTER 16

TALKATIVE

Moreover, I saw in my dream, that as they went on, Faithful happened to look on one side, and saw a man whose name is Talkative, walking at a distance besides them, for in this place, there was room enough for them all to walk. He was a tall man, and somewhat better looking at a distance than near at hand. Faithful addressed Talkative in this manner.

FAITHFUL: *"Friend, where are you going, to the heavenly country?"*

TALKATIVE: *"Yes, I am going to that very place."*

FAITHFUL: *"That is good and I hope we may have your good company."*

TALKATIVE: *"I would be glad to be your companion."*

FAITHFUL: *"Come on, then, let us travel together and let us spend our time discussing profitable things."*

TALKATIVE: *"To talk of good things is very acceptable to me, whether with you, or with any others. I am glad that I have met with you who are inclined to such a good use of time; for, to tell you the truth, most choose to speak of things of no profit and this has been a distress to me."*

FAITHFUL: *"That is indeed a thing to be lamented, for what is more worthy to converse about, than the things of the God of Heaven?"*

TALKATIVE: *"I am very glad to join you, for you speak with conviction. There is nothing so pleasant and so profitable, as to talk of the things of God. For instance, if a man delights to talk of the history or the mystery of things; or if a man loves to talk of miracles, wonders, or signs, where shall he find things recorded so delightfully, and so sweetly penned, as in the Holy Scripture?"*

FAITHFUL: *"That is true, but to be profited by such things in our conversation should be our objective."*

TALKATIVE: *"That is what I said, for to talk of such things is most profitable. In so doing, a man may get knowledge of many things, such as of the vanity of earthly things, and the benefit of heavenly things in general. More particularly, a man may learn the necessity of the new birth; the insufficiency of our works; the need of Christ's righteousness, and so forth. Besides this, a man may learn, by talk, what it is to repent, to believe, to pray, to suffer, and the like. By this also a man may learn what are the great promises and consolations of the Gospel, to his own comfort. Further, by this, a man may learn to refute false opinions, to vindicate the truth, and also to instruct the ignorant."*

FAITHFUL: *"All this is true, and I am glad to hear these things from you."*

TALKATIVE: *"Alas! the lack of such talk is the cause why so few understand the need for faith, and the necessity of a work of grace in their soul, in order to have eternal life, but they ignorantly live in the works of the law, by which a man can by no means obtain the kingdom of Heaven."*

FAITHFUL: *"But, if I may clarify, heavenly knowledge of these things is the gift of God. No man attains them by human effort, or only by talking about them."*

TALKATIVE: *"All this I know very well. For a man can receive nothing, unless it is given him from Heaven. All is by grace, not by works. I could give you a hundred scriptures for the confirmation of this."*

FAITHFUL: *"Well, then, what shall we discuss now?"*

TALKATIVE: *"Whatever you desire. I will talk of heavenly things, or earthly things; moral things, or evangelical things; sacred things, or secular things; past things, or things to come; foreign things, or things at home; essential things, or extraneous things, provided that all is done to our profit."*

Now Faithful began to marvel, and stepping towards Christian, for all this time he had been walking by himself, he softly said to him, *"What a noble companion we have! Surely this man will make a very excellent Pilgrim."*

At this Christian meekly smiled, and said, *"This man, with whom you are so enamored, will beguile twenty people who do not know him, with that tongue of his."*

FAITHFUL: *"Do you know him, then?"*

CHRISTIAN: *"Know him! Yes, better than he knows himself."*

FAITHFUL: *"Tell me, what is he?"*

CHRISTIAN: *"His name is Talkative, and he dwells in our town. I am surprised that you are a stranger to him, yet that is somewhat understandable because our town is so large."*

FAITHFUL: *"Whose son is he and where does he dwell?"*

CHRISTIAN: *"He is the son of Say-well and lived on Prating Row. He is known by all who are acquainted with him, by the name of Talkative on Prating Row. Notwithstanding his fine tongue, he is but a sorry fellow."*

FAITHFUL: *"Well, he seems to be a very charming man."*

CHRISTIAN: *"That he is, to those who do not have a thorough acquaintance with him. He appears good at a distance, but up close he is quite the opposite. Your saying that he is a charming man, brings to my mind what I have observed in the work of the painter, whose pictures look best at a distance, but very near, they are quite unattractive."*

FAITHFUL: *"I almost think you are not serious, because you smiled."*

CHRISTIAN: *"God forbid that I should jest, although I smiled in this matter, or that I should accuse anyone falsely! I will tell you something more about him. Talkative is for any company, and for any talk. Just as he now talks with you, so he will talk when he is at the tavern and the more drink he has in his head, the more talk he has in his mouth. True religion has no place in his heart, or house, or conduct. All his boasted religion lies merely in his tongue."*

FAITHFUL: *"Then I have been greatly deceived by this man."*

CHRISTIAN: *"Deceived! You may be sure of it. Remember the proverb, 'They say, but they do not do.' For the kingdom of God is not in word, but in power. He talks of prayer, of repentance, of faith, and of the new birth, but he only knows how to talk of them. I have been in his family, and have observed him both at home and abroad and I know what I say about him is the truth.*

"His house is as empty of religion, as the white of an egg is of flavor. At his home, there is neither prayer, nor repentance for sin, even the brute animals serve God far better than he. To all who know him, he is the very stain, reproach, and shame of religion! Because of him, God's name is blasphemed at that end of town where he dwells. Thus the people who know him say, 'A saint abroad and a devil at home!' His poor family finds it so, as he is such an ogre. He is so unreasonable with his servants and scolds them so, that they neither know what to do for him, or how to speak to him.

"Men who have any business with him, say that it is better to deal with infidels than with him, for then they would have fairer dealings. For Talkative would go beyond them to defraud, beguile and cheat them.

"He also brings up his sons to follow his steps; and if he finds in any of them a foolish timidity, for so he calls the first appearance of a tender conscience, then he calls them fools and blockheads, and will neither employ them, nor recommend them to others. For my part, I am of the opinion that he has, by his wicked life, caused many to stumble and fall; and will be, if God does not prevent it, the ruin of many more."

FAITHFUL: *"Well, my brother, I am bound to believe you; not only because you say that you know him, but also because, like a Christian, you give honest reports of men. For I know that you do not speak these things out of ill-will, but because it is the truth."*

CHRISTIAN: *"Had I known him no more than you do, I might have thought of him as you did at first. Yes, had Talkative received this report from the enemies of true religion, I would have thought that it was a slander, which often falls from wicked men's lips upon good men's names and professions. But all these things, yes, along with a great many more that I know of, which are just as bad, I can prove him guilty of. Besides, godly men are ashamed of him, they can neither call him brother, nor friend. The very naming of him among them makes them blush, if they know him."*

FAITHFUL: *"Well, I see that saying and doing are two different things, and hereafter I shall better observe this distinction."*

CHRISTIAN: *"They are two different things indeed, and are as diverse as the soul and the body are, for the body without the soul is but a dead carcass. The soul of religion is the practical part: 'Religion that God accepts as pure and faultless is this, to look after orphans and widows in their distress, and to keep oneself from being polluted by the world.' Talkative is not aware of this, he thinks that merely hearing and saying will make a good Christian, and thus he deceives his own soul. Hearing is but as the sowing of the seed. Talking is not sufficient to prove that fruit is indeed in the heart and life. We are sure that at the last day, men shall be judged according to their fruits. It will not be said then, 'Did you believe?' But, 'Were you doers, or talkers only?' All shall be judged accordingly. The end of the world is compared to our harvest and you know men at harvest want nothing but fruit. Not that anything can be accepted by God which is not done in faith, but I only desire to show you how insignificant the profession of Talkative will be at that day."*

FAITHFUL: *"This brings to my mind that chapter of Moses, by which he describes the clean animals for eating. They are such as part the hoof and chew the cud, not which part the hoof only, or which chew the cud only. The rabbit chews the cud, but yet is unclean, because it does not part the hoof. And this truly resembles Talkative; he chews the cud, that is, he seeks knowledge, he chews upon the Word. But he does not divide the hoof, that is, he does not part with the way of sinners. He is therefore unclean."*

CHRISTIAN: *"For all that I know, you have spoken the true Gospel sense of those texts. And I will add another thing: Paul calls some men, yes, and those great talkers too, 'sounding brass and tinkling cymbals.' They are 'things without life, giving sound.' Things without life, that is, without the true faith and grace of the Gospel. Consequently, they are those who shall never be placed in the kingdom of Heaven among those who are the children of life, though their talk is, as if it were, the tongue or voice of an angel."*

FAITHFUL: *"Well, I was not so fond of his company at first, but I am sick of it now! What shall we do to get rid of him?"*

CHRISTIAN: *"Take my advice, and do as I tell you, and you shall find that he will soon be sick of your company too, unless God touches his heart, and converts it."*

FAITHFUL: *"What would you have me to do?"*

CHRISTIAN: *"Why, go to him, and enter into some serious discourse about the power of religion. Then ask him plainly (when he has ap-*

proved of it, for that he will) whether the power of religion is set up in his heart, house, and conduct?"

Then Faithful stepped forward again, and said to Talkative, *"How is it with you?"*

TALKATIVE: *"Very well, thank you. I thought we would have had a great deal of talk by this time."*

FAITHFUL: *"Well, if you desire, we shall begin now. Since you left it with me to state the question, let it be this: How does the saving grace of God reveal itself, when it is in the heart of a man?"*

TALKATIVE: *"I perceive then, that our talk must be about the power of things. Well, it is a very good question, and I shall be willing to answer you. First, where the grace of God is at work in the heart, it causes there a great outcry against sin. Secondly. . ."*

FAITHFUL: *"Wait a moment, let us consider one thing at a time. I think you should rather say: Saving grace reveals itself by inclining the soul to abhor its sin."*

TALKATIVE: *"Why, what difference is there between crying out against sin and abhorring of sin?"*

FAITHFUL: *"O! a great deal. A man may cry out against sin out of principle, but he can only abhor sin by virtue of a holy antipathy against it. I have heard many cry out against sin in the pulpit, who yet can tolerate it well enough in the heart, house, and conduct. Joseph's mistress cried out with a loud voice, as if she had been very holy, but, notwithstanding that, she would have willingly committed adultery with him. Some cry out against sin, even as the mother cries out against her child in her lap, when she calls it a naughty girl and then begins hugging and kissing it."*

TALKATIVE: *"I perceive that you are trying to trap me in my words."*

FAITHFUL: *"No, not I! I am only trying to be precise. But what is the second sign whereby you would prove a work of grace in the heart?"*

TALKATIVE: *"Great knowledge of Gospel mysteries."*

FAITHFUL: *"This sign should have been first, but first or last, it is also false. For knowledge, great knowledge of the mysteries of the Gospel may be obtained and yet there be no work of grace in the soul. Yes, a man may have all knowledge and yet be nothing, and consequently not be a child of God.*

"When Christ said, 'Do you know all these things?' and the disciples had answered, 'Yes', He adds, 'Blessed are you if you do them.' He does not lay the blessing in the knowing of them, but in the doing of them. For there is a head knowledge which is not attended with a corresponding practice: 'He who knows his master's will, and does not carry out those instructions, will be severely punished!' A man may have the knowledge of an angel and yet not be a Christian. Therefore your sign of it is not true.

"Indeed, to know is a thing that pleases talkers and boasters; but to do is that which pleases God. Not that the heart can be good without knowledge; for without knowledge, the heart knows nothing. There are two very distinct kinds of knowledge. There is a knowledge which rests in the bare speculation of things and there is a knowledge which is accompanied with the graces of faith and love; which puts a man upon obeying the will of God from the heart. The first of these will serve the mere talker, but the true Christian is not content without obedience. 'Give me understanding and I shall keep Your law. Yes, I shall observe it with my whole heart!'"

TALKATIVE: *"You are trying to trap me in my words again! This is not pleasing conversation."*

FAITHFUL: *"Well, if you please, propound another sign which shows how this work of grace reveals itself in the heart."*

TALKATIVE: *"Not I, for I see that we shall not agree."*

FAITHFUL: *"Well, if you will not, will you give me permission to do it?"*

TALKATIVE: *"You may if you desire."*

FAITHFUL: *"A work of grace in the soul reveals itself, both to him who has it and to others. To him who has it, thus: It gives him conviction of sin, especially of the defilement of his nature and the sin of unbelief, for the sake of which he is sure to be damned, if he does not find mercy at God's hand, by faith in Jesus Christ. This sight and sense of sin, works in him sorrow and shame for sin. He finds, moreover, that Jesus is revealed as the Savior of the world and the absolute necessity of believing in Him for eternal life, whereby he hungers and thirsts after Him; to which hungerings and thirstings, the promise of salvation is made.*

"Now, according to the strength or weakness of his faith in his Savior, so is his joy and peace, so is his love to holiness, so are his desires to know Him more, and to serve Him in this world.

"But though it reveals itself thus unto him, yet it is but seldom that he is able to conclude that this is a true work of grace. For his corruptions, along with his sin-tainted reason, cause his mind to misjudge in this matter. Therefore, a very sound judgment in him who has this divine work, is required before he can, with certainty, conclude that he has a genuine work of grace in his heart.

"Now to others, this work of grace is thus manifested:

"First, by a heart-felt confession of his faith in Christ.

"Secondly, by a life consistent with that confession. Namely, a life of holiness, heart-holiness, family-holiness, if he has a family, and by conduct-holiness in the world. This work of grace in his heart teaches him, inwardly, to abhor his sin, and himself for his sin, in secret. It also teaches him outwardly to suppress sin in his family, and to promote

holiness in the world, not by talk only, as a hypocrite or talkative person may do, but by a practical obedience, in faith and love, to the Word of God.

"And now, Sir, as to this brief description of the work of grace, and also the manifestation of it, if you have anything to object, then object. But if not, then give me permission to propose a second question to you."

TALKATIVE: *"My part is not now to object, but to hear. Let me, therefore, have your second question."*

FAITHFUL: *"It is this: Do you experience this first part of this description of a saving work of grace? That is, does your life and conduct testify to the same? Or is your religion only in word and tongue, but not in deed and truth? Please, if you decide to answer me, then say no more than you know that God will acknowledge as true. Also, say nothing but what your conscience will justify you in, for it is not he who commends himself who is approved, but he whom the Lord commends. Besides, to say that you are such and such, when your daily conduct, and all your neighbors can tell that you are lying, is great wickedness."*

Talkative then began to blush; but, recovering himself, he thus replied: *"You are now discoursing upon a person's experience and conscience, and appealing to God for justification of what is spoken. I was not expecting this kind of discourse, nor am I disposed to answer such questions, because I am not obligated to do so, unless you have appointed yourself to be my teacher. And even if you should do so, I refuse to make you my judge. But, please, tell me why you ask me such questions?"*

FAITHFUL: *"Because I saw that you were so eager to talk, and because I did not know if you had anything but mere notions. Besides, to tell you the truth, I have heard of you, that you are a man whose religion lies only in talk, and that your conduct gives your profession the lie. They say that you are a blemish among Christians; and that religion fares the worse because of your ungodly conduct; that some already have stumbled because of your wicked ways, and that more are in danger of being destroyed thereby. Your religion and an ale-house, and covetousness, and impurity, and swearing, and lying, and vain company keeping, all join in your conduct. The proverb is true which is said of a harlot, namely, that she is a shame to all women, just so, you are a shame to all professors."*

TALKATIVE: *"Since you are so ready to believe any report, and to judge so rashly as you do, I cannot but conclude that you are some peevish or critical man, not fit to be discoursed with. So I bid you farewell."*

Then Christian came and said to his brother Faithful, *"I told you what would happen, your words and his lusts would not agree! He would rather leave your company, than reform his life. But he is gone, let him go, the loss is no man's but his own. He has saved us the trouble of leaving him, for if he had continued with us, he would have only been a reproach in our company; besides, the apostle says, 'Withdraw yourself from such people.'"*

FAITHFUL: *"But I am glad that we had this little discourse with him, as perhaps he will think of it again. However, I have dealt plainly with him, and so I am clear of his blood if he perishes."*

CHRISTIAN: *"You did well to talk so plainly to him. There is very little of this faithful dealing with men now-a-days and that makes religion a stench in the nostrils of many. For these talkative fools whose religion is only in word, and are debauched and vain in their conduct, (being admitted into the fellowship of the godly), only puzzle the world, blemish Christianity, and grieve the sincere believer. I wish that all men would deal with such hypocrites as you have done; then they would either become sincere believers, or the company of saints would be too hot for them to remain in.*

Then Faithful said,

"How Talkative at first lifts up his plumes!
How bravely does he speak! How he presumes
To drive down all before him! But so soon
As Faithful talks of heart-work, like the moon
That's past the full, into the wane he goes.
And so will all, but he who heart-work knows."

Thus they went on talking of what they had seen along the way, which made their tedious journey easier, for now they were traveling through a wilderness. When they were almost out of this wilderness, Faithful happened to look back, and spotted someone he knew coming after them.

"Oh!" said Faithful to his brother, *"Someone is coming!"*

Then Christian looked, and said: *"It is my good friend Evangelist!"*

"Yes, and my good friend, also." said Faithful, *"For it was he who showed me the way to the gate."*

Now Evangelist caught up to them, and greeted them saying: *"Peace be with you, dearly beloved and peace be with those who were your helpers."*

CHRISTIAN: *"Welcome, welcome, my good friend! The sight of your face brings your past kindness and unwearied laboring for my eternal good, to my remembrance."*

FAITHFUL: *"And a thousand times welcome! Your company, O sweet Evangelist, how desirable it is to us poor Pilgrims!"*

EVANGELIST: *"How has it fared with you, my friends, since the time of our last parting? What have you met with, and how have you conducted yourselves?"*

Then Christian and Faithful told him of all the things which had happened to them along the way and what difficulties they had met with.

EVANGELIST: *"How glad I am, not that you have met with trials, but that you have been victors; and that in spite of many weaknesses, you have continued in the narrow way even to this very day.*

"I am glad both for my own sake and for yours. I have sowed and you have reaped. The day is coming, when both those who sowed and those who reaped shall rejoice together. That is, if you persevere, for in due season you shall reap, if you do not grow weary. The crown is before you, and it is an incorruptible one. So run, that you may obtain it.

"There are some who have set out for this crown, and, after they have gone far for it, have had it taken from them. Hold fast, therefore, what you have, let no man take your crown! You are not yet out of the gunshot reach of the devil. You have not resisted unto blood, striving against sin. Let the kingdom be always before your eyes. Steadfastly believe the things which are not seen; for the things which are seen are temporal, but the things which are not seen are eternal. Let nothing in this world capture your highest affections. Above all, pay attention to your fleshly desires, and your hearts, for they are deceitful above all things, and desperately wicked! Be steadfast, you have all power in Heaven and earth on your side."

Then Christian thanked him for his exhortation, and asked that he would speak further to them for their help the rest of the way. They knew that he was a prophet, and could tell them of things that might happen unto them, and also how they might resist and overcome them.

So Evangelist began as follows: *"My sons, you have heard in the truths of the Gospel, that you must, through many tribulations, enter into the kingdom of Heaven and again, that in every city bonds and afflictions await you. Therefore you cannot expect that you should go long on your pilgrimage without them, in some sort or other. You have found something of the truth of these testimonies already and more will immediately follow.*

"*For now you are almost out of this wilderness, and therefore you will soon come to a town which you will shortly see ahead of you. In that town you will be grievously assaulted by enemies, who will make great attempts to kill you. Be sure that one or both of you must seal the testimony which you hold, with your blood. Be faithful unto death, and the King will give you a crown of life! The one who dies there, although his death will be violent, and his pain perhaps great, will be better off than the other. For he will arrive at the Celestial City the soonest and because he will escape many miseries that the other will meet with along the rest of his journey. But when you have come to the town, and find what I have told you fulfilled, then remember what I have said, and be men of courage, committing yourselves to your faithful Creator, while continuing to do what is right.*"

CHAPTER 17

VANITY FAIR

Then I saw in my dream, that when Christian and Faithful had left the wilderness, they soon saw a town ahead of them named Vanity. At that town there is a fair called Vanity Fair, and it is kept open all the year long. It bears the name of Vanity Fair, because the town where it is held is lighter than vanity and also because all that is sold there is vanity. As is the saying of the wise, *"Vanity of vanities! All is vanity!"*

This fair is no newly-erected business, but a thing of ancient standing. I will show you its origin: Almost five thousand years ago, there were Pilgrims journeying to the Celestial City such as these two honest people. Beelzebub, Apollyon, and Legion, along with their companions, perceived by the path which the Pilgrims made, that their way to the City lay through this town of Vanity. They therefore contrived to set up a fair here in which all sorts of vanity should be sold, and that it should last all the year long.

Therefore all kinds of merchandise are sold at this fair, such as houses, lands, trades, places, honors, preferments, titles, countries, kingdoms, lusts, pleasures; and delights of all sorts, such as harlots, wives, husbands, children, masters, servants, lives, blood, bodies, souls, silver, gold, pearls, precious stones, and what not. Moreover, at this fair are always to be seen juggling, cheats, games, plays, fools, fakes, knaves, and rogues, and that of every kind. Here are to be seen also, and without cost, thefts, murders, adulteries and liars!

As in other fairs of less significance, there are several rows and streets, under their proper names, where such and such wares are vended. So here likewise you have the proper places, namely, countries and kingdoms, where the wares of this fair are soonest to be found. Here is the Britain Row, the French Row, the Italian Row, the Spanish Row, the German Row, where several sorts of vanities are sold. But, as in other fairs, some particular commodity is the chief of all the fair. So the wares of Rome and her merchandise are greatly promoted in this fair, only our English nation, with some others, have taken a dislike thereat.

Now, as I said, the way to the Celestial City lies directly through this town where this lusty fair is kept. He who will go to the Celestial City and yet not go through this town, must need to go out of the world. The King of kings Himself, when here, went through this town to His own country and that upon a fair day as well! Yes, and it was Beelzebub, the chief lord of this fair, who invited Him to buy of his vanities. Yes, he would have made Him lord of the fair, would He have but bowed down to Beelzebub.

Yes, because He was such a person of honor, Beelzebub took Him from street to street, and showed Him all the kingdoms of the world in a short time, that he might, if possible, allure the Blessed One to yield and buy some of his vanities. But He had no desire for this merchandise, and therefore left the town without spending so much as one penny upon these vanities. This fair, therefore, is of ancient standing, and very renowned.

Now these Pilgrims, as I said, had to go through this fair and so they did. And behold, as they entered the fair, all the people in the fair were perplexed, and the town itself was in a hubbub and that for several reasons:

First, The Pilgrims were clothed differently from any who traded in that fair. The people of the fair, therefore, stared at them. Some said they were fools, some said that they were deranged and some said that they were eccentric men.

Secondly, just as they wondered at their apparel, so they likewise were bewildered at their speech, for few could understand what they said. The Pilgrims naturally spoke the language of Canaan, but those who kept the fair were men of this world; so that, from one end of the fair to the other, they seemed to be barbarians to each other.

Thirdly, that which greatly disturbed the peddlers, was that these Pilgrims did not value their wares. They did not desire so much as to look upon them. If the Pilgrims were called upon to buy their merchandise, they would put their fingers in their ears, and cry, *"Turn away my eyes from beholding vanity!"* and look upwards, signifying that their desires and concerns were in Heaven.

Beholding the behavior of the two men, one mockingly asked them, *"What, then, will you buy?"*

But they, looking solemnly upon him, answered, *"We buy the truth!"*

At that, the men of the fair took occasion to despise the Pilgrims all the more, some mocking, some taunting, some speaking reproachfully, and some calling upon others to smite them. At last things came to a hubbub and a great stir in the fair, insomuch that everything was in disorder. So word was soon brought to the lord of the fair, who quickly came down, and delegated some of his most trusty friends to take these Pilgrims, who had so disturbed the fair, into custody.

So the Pilgrims were brought to examination and those who interrogated them asked them from whence they came, and where they were going, and why they were dressed in such an unusual garb?

The two men explained that they were Pilgrims and strangers in the world, and that they were going to their own country, which was the heavenly Jerusalem. They stated that they had given no reason to the men of the town, nor to the peddlers, thus to abuse them, or hinder them in their journey, unless it was, when one asked them what they would buy and they said that they would buy the truth.

But those who were appointed to examine the Pilgrims did not believe them to be anything other than deranged and mad, or else that they had only come to cause trouble at the fair.

Therefore they took them and beat them, and besmeared them with dirt, and then put them into a cage, that they might be made a spectacle to all the men of the fair. Therefore, the Pilgrims lay in the cage for some time, and were made the objects of every man's ridicule or malice, the lord of the fair laughing at all that befell them.

But the Pilgrims, being patient, and not answering insult for insult, but rather a blessing; and returning good words for reproaches, and kindness for injuries done, some men in the fair who were more discerning, and less prejudiced than the rest, began to restrain and blame the examiners for their continual abuses to the Pilgrims.

They, therefore, in angry manner, railed at those who defended the Pilgrims, counting them as bad as the men in the cage. They accused them of being traitors, and said that they should be made partakers of the Pilgrim's punishments.

Those who defended the Pilgrims, replied that for anything they could see, the Pilgrims were quiet and sober-minded, and intended nobody any harm. They also said that there were many who traded in their fair, who were more suitable to be put into the cage, yes, and the stocks also, than were the men that they had abused. Thus, after various arguments had passed on both sides, the Pilgrims all the while behaving themselves very wisely and soberly before them, the men fell to fighting among themselves, and harming one another.

Then these two poor Pilgrims were brought before their examiners again, and charged with being guilty of the hubbub that had been in the fair. So they beat them mercilessly, put them in chains, and led them up and down the fair, for an example and a terror to others, lest any should speak on their behalf, or join themselves unto them.

But Christian and Faithful behaved still more wisely. They received the disgrace and shame which was cast upon them, with so much meekness and patience, that it won several of the men of the fair to their side.

This put the persecuting party into yet a greater rage, insomuch that they sought the death of the two Pilgrims. Therefore they threatened that neither the cage nor the chains were sufficient punishment, but that they should die for the harm they had done, and for deluding the men of the fair.

Then the Pilgrims were thrown into their cage again, until further action would be taken with them. So they put them in, and fastened their feet in the stocks.

Here they remembered what they had heard from their faithful friend Evangelist and were thence encouraged in their way and sufferings, by what he told them would happen to them. They also comforted each other, that he whose lot it was to suffer would have the advantage. Therefore each man secretly wished that he might have the honor of suffering. With much contentment, they committed themselves to the all-wise disposal of Him who rules all things, until they should be otherwise disposed of.

Then at an appointed time, they were brought forth to their trial, and hence to their condemnation. They were brought before their enemies to be arraigned. The Judge's name was Lord Hate-good. Their indictment was one and the same in substance, though somewhat varying in form, the contents whereof were this: *"That they were enemies to, and disturbers of the trade of the city; that they had made disruptions and divisions in the town; and had won some over to their own most dangerous opinions, in contempt of the law of their prince."*

Then Faithful responded: *"I have only set myself against that which has set itself against Him who is higher than the highest. And, as for any disturbance, I made none, being myself a man of peace. Those who were won over to our sentiments, were won by beholding our truth and innocence. They have only turned from the worse, to the better. And as to the king you talk of, since he is Beelzebub, the enemy of our Lord, I defy him and all his minions!"*

Then a proclamation was made, that those who had anything to say for their lord the king against the prisoner at the bar, should now appear and present their evidence. So three witnesses came in, namely, Envy, Superstition, and Pickthank. They were then asked if they knew the prisoner at the bar and what they had to say for their lord the king against him.

So Envy came forth and said: *"My lord, I have known this man a long time, and will attest upon my oath before this honorable bench, that he is . . ."*

Lord Hate-good interrupted: *"Wait! Give him his oath."*

So they swore him in, and Envy continued: *"My lord, this man, notwithstanding his plausible name, is one of the vilest men in our country! He neither regards prince nor people, law nor custom, but does all that he can to influence others with certain of his disloyal notions, which he calls principles of faith and holiness. And, in particular, I myself heard him once affirm that Christianity and the customs of our town of Vanity, were diametrically opposite, and could not be reconciled. By saying this, my lord, he at once condemns both all our laudable doings and us in the doing of them."*

Then the Judge, Lord Hate-good, said to him, *"Have you any more to say?"*

ENVY: *"My lord, I could say much more, but this would be tedious to the court. Yet, if need be, when the other gentlemen have given forth their evidence, if anything shall be lacking which would condemn Faithful, I will then enlarge my testimony against him."*

So Envy was told to stand by. Then they called Superstition, and asked him what he could say for their lord the king against Faithful. Then they swore him in and so he began.

SUPERSTITION: *"My lord, I have no great acquaintance with this man, nor do I desire to have any further knowledge of him! However, this I know from a discourse which I had with him the other day, that he is a very pestilent fellow! He said that our religion was worthless, and could by no means please God and therefore we worship in vain, are yet in our sins, and shall finally be damned!"*

Then Pickthank was sworn in, and ordered to say what he knew on behalf of their lord the king, against the prisoner at the bar.

PICKTHANK: *"My lord, and all you gentlemen. I have known this fellow for a long time, and have heard him speak things that ought not to be spoken! He has railed against our noble prince Beelzebub, and has spoken contemptibly of his honorable friends, Lord Old Man, Lord Carnal Delight, Lord Luxurious, Lord Desire of Vain Glory, old Lord Lechery, Sir Having Greedy, along with all the rest of our nobility!*

"He has said, moreover, that if all men were of his mind, that these noblemen would all be run out of town. He has also not been afraid to rail at you, my lord, who is now appointed to be his judge, calling you an ungodly villain, along with many other such vilifying terms, with which he has bespattered most of the aristocracy of our town!"

When Pickthank had told his tale, the Judge directed his speech to the prisoner at the bar, saying, *"You renegade, heretic, and traitor! Have you heard what these honest gentlemen have witnessed against you?"*

FAITHFUL: *"May I speak a few words in my own defense?"*

LORD HATE-GOOD: *"You scoundrel! You do not deserve to live, but to be slain immediately right where you are standing! Yet, so that all men may see our gentleness towards you, let us hear what you, vile rebel, have to say."*

FAITHFUL: *"First. I say in answer to what Mr. Envy has spoken, that I never said anything but this: That whatever rules, or laws, or customs,* or people, which are contrary to the Word of God, are diametrically opposite to Christianity. If I have said anything amiss in this, then convince me of my error, and I will make my recantation before you.

"Secondly, to answer Mr. Superstition and his charge against me, I said only this: That a divine faith is required in the worship of God, and there can be no divine faith without a Divine revelation of the will of God. Therefore, whatever is thrust into the worship of God which does not agree with Divine revelation, is nothing but man's vain religion, and will never lead to eternal life.

"Thirdly, in answer to what Mr. Pickthank has charged, I did say that the prince of this town, with all his rabblement and attendants, are more fit for being in Hell, than in this town and country! And so, may the Lord have mercy upon me!"

Then Judge Hate-good called to the jury, who all this while stood by to hear and observe: "Gentlemen of the jury, you see this man about whom so great an uproar has been made in this town. You have also heard what these worthy gentlemen have witnessed against him, and have heard his reply and confession. It lies now in your power to either hang him, or save his life. Yet first, I think it necessary to instruct you concerning our law.

"There was an Act made in the days of Pharaoh the Great, servant of our prince, that lest those of a contrary religion should multiply and grow too strong for him, their males should be thrown into the river.

"There was also an Act made in the days of Nebuchadnezzar the Great, another of our prince's servants, that whoever would not fall down and worship his golden image, should be thrown into a fiery furnace.

"There was also an Act made in the days of Darius, that whoever called upon any god but him, should be cast into the lions' den.

"Now this rebel here, has broken the substance of all of these laws, not *only in thought (which is not to be tolerated) but also in word and deed, which is absolutely intolerable!*

"For Pharaoh's law was made upon a supposition, to prevent mischief, no crime being yet apparent. Yet here is an obvious crime. And as for the laws of Nebuchadnezzar and Darius, you plainly see that Faithful openly disputes against our religion! For the treason which he has confessed, he deserves to die!"

Then the jury went out, their names were, Mr. Blind-man, Mr. No-good, Mr. Malice, Mr. Love-lust, Mr. Live-loose, Mr. Heady, Mr. High-mind, Mr. Enmity, Mr. Liar, Mr. Cruelty, Mr. Hate-light, and Mr. Implacable. Each of the jury gave their verdict against Faithful and unanimously concluded to charge him as guilty before Lord Hate-good.

First, Mr. Blind-man, the foreman, exclaimed, *"I see clearly that this man is a heretic!"*

Then Mr. No-good added, *"Away with such a fellow from the earth!"*

"Absolutely!" said Mr. Malice, *"For I hate the very looks of him!"*

Then Mr. Love-lust remarked, *"I could never stomach him!"*

"Neither could I!" added Mr. Live-loose, *"For he would always be condemning my way!"*

"Hang him, hang him!" Mr. Heady demanded.

"He is a sorry base fellow!" exclaimed Mr. High-mind.

"My heart revolts against him!" sniveled Mr. Enmity.

"He is a rogue!" Mr. Liar declared.

"Hanging is too good for him!" snarled Mr. Cruelty.

"Let us dispatch him out of the way!" snapped Mr. Hate-light.

Then Mr. Implacable exclaimed, *"I would not be reconciled to him for all the world! Therefore, let us immediately charge him to be deserving of death!"*

And so they did. Therefore Faithful was condemned at once. He was taken from the court, and back to his cage and from there, he was to be put to the most cruel death that could be invented.

They then brought him out, to punish him according to their law. First, they scourged him, then they buffeted him, then they lanced his flesh with knives! After that, they stoned him with stones, then pierced him with their swords. Last of all, they burned him to ashes at the stake! Thus Faithful came to his end.

Now I saw that behind the multitude, there was a chariot with horses waiting for Faithful, who, as soon as his adversaries had murdered him, was taken up into it. He was immediately carried up through the clouds, with the sound of the trumpet, to the nearest way to the Celestial Gate.

But as for Christian, he had some reprieve, and was sent back to the prison and remained there for a time.

Then He who overrules all things, having power over the rage of His enemies in His own hand, so brought it about that Christian escaped from them, and went on his way. As he went, he sang,

> *"Well, Faithful, you have faithfully professed,*
> *Unto your Lord, with Whom you shall be blessed,*
> *When faithless ones, with all their vain delights,*
> *Are crying out under their Hellish plights,*
> *Sing, Faithful, sing and let your name survive;*
> *For, though they killed you, you are yet alive!"*

Now I saw in my dream, that Christian did not journey alone, for there was one named Hopeful (being made so by beholding Christian and Faithful in their words, behaviors and sufferings at the Fair), who joined with him. Entering into a brotherly covenant, Hopeful told Christian that he would be his companion. He also told Christian that there were many more from Vanity Fair, who would be following after them.

Thus, one died to bear testimony to the truth, while another rises out of his ashes, to be a companion with Christian in his pilgrimage.

CHAPTER 18

MR. BY-ENDS

So I saw that quickly after they left the Fair, they overtook one who was ahead of them, whose name was By-ends. They said to him, *"What country are you from, Sir and how far do you intend to go this way?"*

He told them, that he came from the town of Fair-speech, and he was going to the Celestial City, but, he did not tell them his name.

"From Fair-speech!" Christian exclaimed. *"Are there any godly people living there?"*

"Yes," said By-ends, *"I certainly hope so!"*

"Please, Sir, what may I call you?" Christian said.

BY-ENDS: *"I am a stranger to you and you to me. If you are going this way, I shall be glad to have your company; but if not, I must be content to travel alone."*

"This town of Fair-speech," Christian said, *"I have heard of. As I remember, they say that it is a wealthy place."*

BY-ENDS: *"Yes, I will assure you that it is and I have many very rich kindred there!"*

CHRISTIAN: *"Who are your kindred there, if I may be so bold to ask."*

BY-ENDS: *"Almost the whole town! In particular, my Lord Turn-about, my Lord Time-server, my Lord Fair-speech, from whose ancestors that town first took its name, also Mr. Smooth-man, Mr. Facing-both-*

ways, and Mr. Any-thing. The parson of our parish, Mr. Two-tongues, is my mother's own brother! To tell you the truth, I have become a gentleman of good quality. My great grandfather was but a waterman, looking one way and rowing another; and I got most of my estate by the same occupation."

CHRISTIAN: *"Are you a married man?"*

BY-ENDS: *"Yes, my wife is a very virtuous woman and the daughter of a virtuous woman. She was my Lady Feigning's daughter, therefore she came from a very honorable family. She has arrived to such a height of good breeding, that she knows how to behave towards all kinds of people, whether prince or peasant.*

"It is true that we somewhat differ in religion from those of the stricter sort, but only in two small points:

First, we never strive against wind and tide;

Secondly, we are always most zealous when religion goes in silver slippers. We love to walk with religion in the street, if the sun shines, and the people applaud it."

Then Christian stepped a little aside to his fellow Hopeful, saying, *"I am thinking that this is Mr. By-ends from the town of Fair-speech and if so, we have as bad a knave in our company, as dwells in all these parts."*

Then Hopeful replied, *"Ask him again, I think he should not be ashamed of his own name."*

So Christian came up to By-ends again, and said, *"Sir, you talk as if one could serve both God and Mammon at the same time. I think I know who you are, is not your name Mr. By-ends, of the town of Fair-speech?"*

BY-ENDS: *"This is not my name, but indeed it is a nickname that is given to me by some who do not like me. I must be content to bear it as a reproach, as other good men have borne reproach before me."*

CHRISTIAN: *"But did you ever give an occasion for men to call you by this name?"*

BY-ENDS: *"Never, never! The worst that I ever did, was that I always had the wisdom to go along with the current ways of the times, whatever they were. I was always lucky enough to prosper thereby. But if the malicious cast such reproachful names upon me, then let me count them a blessing."*

CHRISTIAN: *"I thought, indeed, that you were the By-ends that I have heard of and I think that this name belongs more properly to you, than you are willing to admit."*

BY-ENDS: *"Well, if you thus think so, I cannot help that. I am sure that you shall find me to be a good companion, if you agree to take me along with you."*

CHRISTIAN: *"If you will come with us, then you must go against the wind and tide, which, I perceive, is against your desires. You must also own religion when in his rags, as well as when in his silver slippers. You must stand with him, too, when he is bound in iron chains, as well as when he walks the streets with applause."*

BY-ENDS: *"You will not be my judge, nor impose your views upon me! Allow me to do as I think best and let me go with you."*

CHRISTIAN: *"You shall not go a step further with us, unless you intend to do as we proposed!"*

Then By-ends retorted, *"I shall never desert my old principles, since they are both harmless and profitable! If I may not go with you, then I must do as I did before you caught up with me, travel by myself, until I meet with someone who will be glad for my company."*

Now I saw in my dream, that Christian and Hopeful forsook Mr.

By-ends, and kept their distance ahead of him. Looking back, they saw three men following him. As they came up to him, he made a very low bow as he greeted them and they gave him a compliment.

The men's names were Mr. Hold-the-world, Mr. Money-love, and Mr. Save-all. They all were men that Mr. By-ends had formerly been acquainted with, for in their youth they were school-fellows, and were taught by one Mr. Gripeman, a school-master in Love-gain, which is a market town in the county of Coveting, in the north. This schoolmaster taught them the art of prospering, either by violence, deceit, flattery, lying, or by putting on a pretense of religion. These four gentlemen had attained much of the art of their master, so that each of them could have run such a school themselves.

Well, when they had thus greeted each other, Mr. Money-love said to Mr. By-ends, *"Who are those two people on the road before us?"*, for Christian and Hopeful were yet within view.

BY-ENDS: *"They are a couple of distant countrymen, who, in their strange manner, are going on pilgrimage."*

MR. MONEY-LOVE: *"Alas! Why did they not wait, that we might have had their good company? For we are all going on a pilgrimage."*

BY-ENDS: *"Indeed we are, but the men ahead of us are so rigid, and love their own notions so much, and so lightly esteem the opinions of others, that let a man be ever so godly, yet if he does not agree with them in all things, they will thrust him out of their company."*

MR. SAVE-ALL: *"That is bad. We read of some who are overly righteous and such men's rigidness prevails with them to judge and condemn all others but themselves. Please tell me what, and how many, were the things wherein you differed from them?"*

BY-ENDS: *"Why, after their headstrong manner, they conclude that it is their duty to push ahead on their journey in all weathers, but I am for waiting for more favorable winds and tides. They are for risking all for God at any moment, but I am in favor of taking all advantages to secure my life and estate. They are for clinging to their beliefs, even though all other men are against them, but I am for religion only so far as the times, and my safety, will bear it. They are for religion even when it is contemptible and in rags, but I am for religion only when it walks in golden slippers, in the sunshine, and with applause."*

MR. HOLD-THE-WORLD: *"Exactly, good Mr. By-ends! For my part, I count him to be a fool, who, having the liberty to keep what he has, shall be so unwise as to lose it. Let us be wise as serpents! It is best to make hay when the sun shines. You see how the bee lies still all winter, and bestirs itself only when it can have profit with pleasure. God sometimes sends rain and sometimes sunshine. If they are such fools to go through the storm, yet let us be content to only travel in fair weather.*

"For my part, the religion that I like the best, allows us to have God's earthly blessings. For it is only reasonable, that since God has bestowed upon us the good things of this life, that He would have us keep them for His sake. Abraham and Solomon grew rich in religion. And Job says, that a good man shall lay up gold as dust. But we must never be as the men ahead of us, if they are as you have described them."

MR. SAVE-ALL: *"I think that we are all agreed on this matter and therefore we need no more discussion about it."*

MR. MONEY-LOVE: *"Indeed, we need no more discussion about this matter! For the one who believes neither Scripture nor reason and you see that we have both on our side, neither knows his own liberty, nor seeks his own safety."*

BY-ENDS: *"My brethren, as you know, we are all going on pilgrimage. Therefore to divert our attention from base things, allow me to propound this question unto you: Suppose a man, a minister, or a tradesman, should have an opportunity before him to obtain the good things of this life. Yet he cannot obtain them unless, in appearance at least, he becomes extraordinarily zealous in some points of religion which he had no interest in beforehand. May he not use such religion to attain his end and still be a righteous and honest man?"*

MR. MONEY-LOVE: *"I see the bottom of your question. With these gentlemen's permission, I will endeavor to give you an answer. Firstly, to speak to your question as it concerns a minister himself. Suppose there is a minister, a worthy man, who had only a very small salary, but desires a greater and more lucrative income. He now has an opportunity of getting it, but only by being more studious, by preaching more frequently and zealously; and, because the disposition of the people requires it, by altering some of his principles. For my part, I see no problem with a minister doing this, yes, and a great deal more besides and still remain an honest man. I say this, for the following reasons:*

"First, it cannot be denied that his desire for a larger income is lawful, since it is put before him by Providence. So then, he may strive to obtain it, without his conscience raising any questions.

"Secondly, his desire for a more lucrative income makes him more studious, a more zealous preacher, and so forth, thus making him a better man. Yes, it also makes him improve his natural abilities, which is according to the mind of God.

"Thirdly, as for his complying with the disposition of his people, by altering some of his principles so that he may better serve them, this indicates:

(1). That he is of a self-denying temperament.

(2). That he is of a sweet and winning demeanor.

(3). That he is more fit for the ministerial office.

"Finally, I conclude then, that a minister who changes a small salary for a greater one, should not, for so doing, be judged as a covetous per-

son. Rather, since he has improved his abilities and industry, he should be counted as a worthy minister who has expanded his opportunities to do good.

"And now to the second part of your question, which concerns the tradesman you mentioned. Suppose such a one has but a poor shop, but by becoming religious, he may increase his market, get more and far better customers to his shop, and perhaps even get a rich wife. For my part, I see no problem why this may not be lawfully done. I say this, for the following reasons:

"First, to become religious is a virtue, regardless of whatever reason he becomes so.

"Secondly, nor is it unlawful to get a rich wife, or more customers to his shop.

"Lastly, the man who gets these by becoming religious, gets that which is good, from those who are good, by becoming good himself! So then, here is a good wife, and good customers, and good gain and all these just by becoming religious, which is good! Therefore, to become religious to get all these, is a good and profitable endeavor."

This answer, made by Mr. Money-love to Mr. By-end's question, was highly applauded by them all. They therefore concluded that it was most wholesome, advantageous and unable to be contradicted. Because Christian and Hopeful had opposed Mr. By-ends previously, they jointly agreed to challenge them with the same question as soon as they caught up with them, for they were still within sight. But they decided that old Mr. Hold-the-world and not Mr. By-ends, should propose the question to them. For they supposed that Christian and Hopeful's discussion with Mr. Hold-the-world would be less heated.

So they called after Christian and Hopeful and they stopped and stood still until the four men caught up to them. After a short greeting, Mr. Hold-the-world put forth the question to Christian and Hopeful, and asked them to answer it if they could.

CHRISTIAN: *"Even a babe in religion may answer ten thousand such questions. For if it is unlawful to follow Christ for mere loaves, then how much more abominable it is to attempt to make Him and religion into an instrument to gain and enjoy the world. Nor do we find any other than heathen, hypocrites, devils, and sorcerers, who are of this opinion.*

"First, the Heathen are of this religion. For when Hamor and Shechem desired to obtain the daughter and the cattle of Jacob, they were told that there was no way for them to procure them but by becoming circumcised. So they reasoned, 'Will not their livestock and their property all become ours? Therefore let us consent to their request.'

"Jacob's daughter and his cattle were that which they sought to obtain and their religion was the stalking-horse they made use of in attempting to procure them. You may read the whole story in Genesis 34:20-23.

"Secondly, the hypocritical Pharisees were also of this religion. Long prayers were their pretense, but to get widows' houses was their intention; and greater damnation was their judgment from God.

"Thirdly, Judas the devil was also of this religion. He was religious for the money-bag, that he might get gain; but he was lost, cast away, and became the very son of perdition.

"Fourthly, Simon the sorcerer was of this religion also, for he desired the power of the Holy Spirit so that he might make gain. His condemnation from Peter's mouth was suitable: 'May your money perish with you, because you thought you could purchase the gift of God with money!'

"Fifthly, I am also mindful that the man who takes up religion for the world, will also throw away religion for the world. For as surely as

Judas contrived to obtain the world by becoming religious, so just as surely he also sold his Master and religion for money.

"Therefore to answer the question affirmatively, as you have done; and to accept such an answer as satisfactory, is both heathenish, hypocritical, and devilish; and your reward will be according to your works!"

Then they stood staring at each other, not knowing how to answer Christian, so there was a long silence among them. Therefore Mr. By-ends and his friends began to lag behind, so that Christian and Hopeful might travel on ahead of them.

Hopeful approved of the soundness of Christian's answer. Then Christian said to his fellow-traveler, *"If these men cannot stand before the sentence of men, then what will they do when they stand before the sentence of God? And if they are speechless when dealt with by vessels of clay, then how will they respond when they are rebuked by the flames of the devouring fire?"*

CHAPTER 19

THE HILL LUCRE

Then Christian and Hopeful traveled on ahead of the others, until they came to a pleasant meadow, called Ease, where they journeyed with much delight. As the meadow was only a short length, they quickly traveled over it.

Now at the farthest side of that meadow was a little hill called Lucre and in that hill was a silver mine. Because this was so rare, some of those who had formerly gone that way had turned aside to see it, but going too near to the brink of the pit, and the ground being unstable under them, it broke away, and they were killed. Some others were so injured that they could not, to their dying day, be recovered.

Then I saw in my dream, that a little way off the road, near the silver mine stood a gentleman named Demas. He called out to passing travelers to come and see. He beckoned to Christian and Hopeful, *"Ho! turn aside here and I will show you something quite special!"*

CHRISTIAN: *"What is so deserving as to turn us out of the way to see it?"*

DEMAS: *"Here is a silver mine and some are digging in it for treasure. If you come, with a little effort you may be richly rewarded."*

Then Hopeful responded, *"Let us go and see!"*

"Not I," Christian cautioned, *"I have heard of this place before. Many have been destroyed there. And besides that, worldly treasure is a snare to those who seek it, for it hinders them in their pilgrimage."*

Then Christian called to Demas, *"Is not the place dangerous? Has it not hindered many in their pilgrimage?"*

DEMAS: *"It is not very dangerous, except to those who are careless"*, but he blushed as he spoke.

Then Christian said to Hopeful, *"Let us not turn a step out of the way, but still keep on our path."*

HOPEFUL: *"I assure you, that when By-ends arrives here, if he has the same invitation as we did, that he will turn aside and go to Hill Lucre."*

CHRISTIAN: *"No doubt about that, for his principles lead him that way. A hundred to one, that he dies there!"*

Then Demas called again, saying, *"Will you not even come over and look?"*

Then Christian firmly answered, *"Demas, you are an enemy to the right ways of the Lord. You have been already condemned for your own turning aside. Why are you seeking to bring us into the same condemnation? Furthermore, if we turn aside at all, then our Lord the King will certainly hear of it; and rather than standing with boldness before Him, we would instead be put to shame."*

Then Demas cried out that he was one of their kinsmen; and that if they would only tarry a little, he also would walk with them.

Then Christian asked, *"What is your name? Is it not Demas?"*

DEMAS: *"Yes, my name is Demas. I am the son of Abraham."*

CHRISTIAN: *"I know you! Gehazi was your great-grandfather, Judas was your father and you are treading in their steps. You are using a devilish prank! Your father was hanged as a traitor and you deserve no better recompense. Assure yourself, that when we come to the King, we will tell Him of your behavior."*

Thus they continued on their way.

By this time By-ends and his companions had come within sight and they, at the first beckoning, went over to Demas. Now, whether they fell into the pit by looking over its brink, or whether they went down to dig in the silver mine, or whether they were smothered in the bottom by the fumes which commonly arise, of these things I am not certain. Yet this I observed, that they were never again seen in the way.

Then Christian sang:

> *"By-ends and silver Demas both agree;*
> *One calls, the other runs, that he may be*
> *A sharer in his lucre; so these do*
> *Take up in this world, and no further go."*

Now I saw that, just on the other side of this plain, the Pilgrims came to a place where an old monument stood near the side of the highway. Upon seeing it, they were both concerned because of the strangeness of its form, for it seemed to them as if it had been a woman transformed into the shape of a pillar.

They therefore stood looking upon it and for a time, could not tell what they should make of it. At last Hopeful spotted an inscription in an unusual dialect written above the monument; but being no scholar, he called to Christian (who was more learned) to see if he could understand the meaning. So Christian came, and after examining the letters, he found its meaning to be: *"Remember Lot's wife!"*

After reading it to Hopeful, they both concluded that this was the pillar of salt which Lot's wife had been turned into, for her looking back with a covetous heart, when she was fleeing Sodom for safety. This sudden and amazing sight prompted the following discourse.

CHRISTIAN: *"Ah, my brother, this is a timely warning! It came prov-*

identially to us after Demas' invitation to come over to view the Hill Lucre. Had we gone as he desired, and as you were first inclined to do, my brother, we ourselves would probably have been made like this woman, a spectacle to behold, for those who come after."

HOPEFUL: *"I am sorry that I was so foolish, and am astonished that I am not now as Lot's wife, for what is the difference between her sin and mine? She only looked back, but I had a desire to go and see. Let God's grace be adored and let me be ashamed, that such a thing should ever have been in my heart."*

CHRISTIAN: *"Let us take notice of what we have seen here, for our help in times to come. This woman escaped one judgment, for she escaped the destruction of Sodom; yet she was destroyed by another judgment, as we see that she was turned into a pillar of salt."*

HOPEFUL: *"True, and she serves both as a warning and an example to us. She is a warning, in that we should shun her sin, or receive her judgment. Korah, Dathan, and Abiram, along with the two hundred and fifty men who perished in their sin, are also an example for others to beware.*

"But above all, I am astonished at one thing, how Demas and his fellows can so confidently stand looking for that treasure, which Lot's wife, just for looking behind her was turned into a pillar of salt. For we do not read that she stepped one foot out of the way! More especially so, since the judgment which overtook her, made her a monument within sight of where they are. For they cannot but see her, if they would only lift up their eyes."

CHRISTIAN: *"It is a thing to be amazed at. It argues that their hearts have grown so hardened in this case. I cannot tell who to compare them to so aptly, as to those who pick pockets in the presence of the judge, or would rob purses under the gallows.*

"It is said of the men of Sodom, that they were exceedingly wicked and

sinful before the Lord, that is, in His eyesight; and notwithstanding the kindnesses which He had shown them, for the land of Sodom was like the garden of Eden at that time. This, therefore, more provoked Him, and made their punishment as hot as the fire of the Lord out of Heaven could make it. It is most rationally to be concluded, that those who shall sin in God's sight, although such examples are continually set before them to caution them to the contrary, must be partakers of the most severe judgments!"

HOPEFUL: *"Doubtless you have spoken the truth. What a mercy it is, that neither you, nor especially I, were made to be similar examples as that forsaken woman! This gives us an occasion to thank God, to fear Him, and always to remember Lot's wife."*

CHAPTER 20

BY-PATH MEADOW

I saw, then, that they went on their way to a pleasant river, which King David called *"the river of God"*, but the apostle John called *"the river of the water of life."*

Now their way lay along the bank of the river. Here, therefore, Christian and his companion walked with great delight, they drank of the water of the river, which was pleasant and enlivening to their weary spirits. On the banks of both sides of this river, were green trees which bore all kinds of fruit, which the Pilgrims were also much pleased with. Furthermore, the leaves of the trees were also good for medicine. They prevented sicknesses and other diseases that are common to traveling Pilgrims.

On both sides of the river there was a meadow which remained green all the year long and was intricately beautified with lilies. In this meadow they lay down and slept, for here they could sleep in safety. When they awoke, they again gathered fruit from the trees, and drank of the water of the river and once more lay down to sleep. Thus they did for several days and nights.

Then they sang:

> *"Behold how these crystal streams do glide,*
> *To comfort Pilgrims by the highway side;*
> *The meadows green, besides their fragrant smell,*
> *Yield dainties for them, and he who can tell*

What pleasant fruit, yes, leaves, these trees do yield,
Will soon sell all, that he may buy this field."

So when they were prepared to travel on, for they were not as yet at their journey's end, again they ate and drank, and departed.

Now, I beheld in my dream, that they had not journeyed far when their path separated away from the river. This saddened them, but they dared not depart from their course. Now their path became rough and their feet were tender because of their long travels. So they became discouraged because of the difficulty of the way and wished for an easier route.

Now, just ahead of them on the left side of the road, was a field named By-path Meadow, which could be entered by a stile.

Then Christian said to Hopeful, *"If this meadow lies alongside our way, then let us go over into it."*

So he went to the stile to see and behold, there was a path on the other side of the fence which ran alongside their way.

"It is just as I desired! Here is an easy-going way, come, good Hopeful, and let us go over!" Christian exclaimed.

HOPEFUL: *"But what if this easy path should lead us out of the way?"*

CHRISTIAN: *"That is not likely. Look, it goes right alongside our pathway."*

So Hopeful, being persuaded by his fellow, left the path and followed Christian over the stile. Once in the meadow, they found it very easy for their feet.

Looking ahead of them, they saw a man named Vain-confidence. So they called after him, and asked him where this path led.

"To the Celestial Gate," he replied.

"*Look,*" Christian said to Hopeful, "*did I not tell you so? Now you see that we are in the right path!*"

So they followed Vain-confidence, and he went on ahead of them. But, behold, as the night came on, it grew very dark and they lost sight of him.

Vain-confidence, not seeing the way before him, fell into a deep pit and was dashed to pieces! This pit was purposely made by the king of those grounds in order to catch vain-glorious fools.

Now Christian and Hopeful heard him fall. So they called to him, but there was no answer. They only heard someone groaning.

Then Hopeful asked, "*Where are we now?*"

Christian did not answer, fearing that he had led Hopeful out of the right way.

It now began to rain, with thundering and lightening, in a most dreadful manner and the water was rising around them.

Then Hopeful groaned within himself, saying, "*O that I had remained on my way!*"

CHRISTIAN: "*Who could have thought that this path would have led us out of the way?*"

HOPEFUL: "*I was afraid of that at the very first, and therefore gave you a gentle caution. I would have spoken plainer, but for the fact that you are older than I.*"

CHRISTIAN: "*Good brother, do not be offended. I am sorry I have brought you out of the way, and that I have put you into such imminent danger. Please forgive me, I did not do it with an evil intent.*"

HOPEFUL: "*Be comforted, my brother, for I do forgive you. We must believe that this too shall be for our good.*"

CHRISTIAN: *"I am glad that you are such a merciful brother. We must not stay here, let us try to go back again."*

HOPEFUL: *"But, good brother, let me go first."*

CHRISTIAN: *"No, if you please, let me go ahead, so that if there is any danger, I may meet it first, because by my guidance we have both gone out of the way."*

HOPEFUL: *"No, you shall not go first; for your mind is troubled, and you may lead us out of the way again."*

Then, for their encouragement, they heard the voice of one saying, *"Set your heart toward the highway, even the way by which you came; turn back."*

But by this time the waters had greatly risen, so the way of going back was very dangerous. Then Christian realized that it is easier to go out of the right way, than to get back into it.

So they attempted to go back, but it was so dark, and the flood was so high, that they almost drowned nine or ten times. Neither could they, using all their skill, get back to the stile that night. At last, finding a little shelter, they sat down there. Being weary, they fell asleep until the day-break.

CHAPTER 21

DOUBTING CASTLE

Not far from the place where they slept, there was a castle called Doubting Castle, whose owner was Giant Despair. It was on his grounds that the Pilgrims were now sleeping.

Giant Despair, getting up early in the morning, and walking up and down in his fields, caught Christian and Hopeful asleep on his grounds. Then, with a grim and surly voice, he ordered them to awake. He asked them where they came from and what they were doing on his grounds.

They told him that they were Pilgrims, and that they had lost their way.

Then the Giant declared, *"You are trespassing on my grounds and therefore you must come along with me!"*

So they were forced to go with him, because he was stronger than they. The Pilgrims had but little to say, for they knew themselves to be at fault. The Giant therefore drove them before him, and put them into a very dark, nasty and stinking dungeon of his castle.

Here then they lay from Wednesday morning until Saturday night, without one bit of bread, or drop of water, or light, or anyone to help them. Therefore they were in a dreadful state, being far from friends and assistance.

Now in this place Christian had a double sorrow, for it was through his ill-advised counsel that they were brought into this distress.

Now, Giant Despair had a wife whose name was Diffidence. When he had gone to bed, he told his wife what he had done, namely, that he had taken a couple of prisoners, and cast them into his dungeon for trespassing on his grounds. He also asked her what he should further do to them.

So she asked him who they were, where they came from, and where they were going and he told her. Then she counseled him that when he awoke in the morning, he should beat them without mercy.

So, when he arose in the morning, he took a large crab-tree cudgel, and went down into the dungeon to them. He began to berate them as if they were dogs, even though they never gave him any reason for doing so.

Then he fell upon them, and beat them mercilessly with the cudgel and in such a way that they were not able to defend themselves or escape the Giant's clutches.

This done, he withdrew and left them there to commiserate their wretchedness, and to mourn over their distress. So all that day they spent the time in nothing but sighs and bitter lamentations.

The next night, Diffidence, talking further with her husband about the Pilgrims, and finding out that they were still alive, told him to advise them to kill themselves.

So when morning came, he went to them in the same surly manner as before. Perceiving them to be in much pain because of the beating that he had given them the day before, he told them that since they were never going to get out of that dungeon, the best thing for them would be to kill themselves, either with knife, noose or poison. *"For why,"* he questioned, *"should you choose life, seeing it is attended with so much bitterness?"*

But the Pilgrims begged him to let them go. With that, he looked harshly at them. Rushing upon them, he would have doubtless made an end of them, except that he fell into one of his fits, for he sometimes fell into fits in sunshiny weather, and lost the use of his hands for a time. Therefore he withdrew, and left them to consider what they would do. Then the prisoners discussed whether it was best to take his counsel or not; and thus they began to discourse:

CHRISTIAN: *"Brother, what shall we do? The life that we now live is miserable. For my part, I do not know what is best, to live like this, or to kill ourselves. The grave seems better to me than living in this dungeon, only to be oppressed by this Giant!"*

HOPEFUL: *"Indeed, our present condition is dreadful and death would be far more welcome to me than to live like this forever! Yet let us consider that the Lord of the country to which we are going has said, 'You shall not murder.' We are not to take another man's life, much more, then, are we forbidden to take the Giant's counsel to kill ourselves. Besides, he who kills another, can but commit murder upon his body. But for one to commit suicide, is to kill both body and soul at once! Moreover, my brother, you talk of ease in the grave, but have you forgotten that there is a Hell where all murderers go? For no murderer has eternal life!*

"And let us consider, again, that all circumstances are not in the hand of Giant Despair. Others, so far as I understand, have been captured by him, as well as we, yet they have escaped out of his clutches. Who knows, but that the God who made the world, may cause Giant Despair to die? Or that, at some time or other, he may forget to lock us in? Or that he may have another one of his fits when he is with us, and may lose the use of his limbs? If that ever happens, I am resolved to take courage, and try my utmost to escape his grasp. I was a fool that I did not try to do it before. However, my brother, let us be patient, and endure for a while. The time may come in which we may be released, but let us not be our own murderers!"

With these words, Hopeful pacified the mind of his brother. So they continued together in their sad and doleful condition.

Now, towards evening, the Giant went down into the dungeon again, to see if his prisoners had taken his advice, but when he arrived there, he found them still living. Yet they were barely alive, for they lacked bread and water. Because of the wounds they received when he beat them, they could do little more than breathe. Seeing that they were still alive, Giant Despair fell into a furious rage. He told them, that since they had not taken his advice, it would now be worse with them than if they had never been born. With that, he departed.

At this they trembled greatly, and Christian fell into a swoon. Upon reviving, they renewed their discussion about the Giant's advice and whether or not it was best to follow it. Once again, Christian seemed to favor suicide.

Hopeful then responded: *"My brother, remember how valiant you have been up to this time! Apollyon could not crush you, nor could all that you heard, or saw, or experienced in the Valley of the Shadow of Death. What hardship and terror you have already gone through, but now are you so fearful?*

"You see that I, a far weaker man by nature than yourself, am in this dungeon with you. The Giant has wounded me as well as you and has also cut off my bread and water and with you I mourn in this dark dungeon. Let us exercise a little more patience. Remember how courageous you were at Vanity Fair, and were neither afraid of the fetters, nor the cage, nor of a bloody death. Therefore let us bear up with patience as well as we can, for suicide is shameful, and unfitting for a Christian."

Now, night having come, and the Giant and his wife being in bed, she asked him if the prisoners had taken his counsel. To which he replied, *"They are sturdy rogues and choose rather to bear all hardship, than to kill themselves."*

So she then said, *"Take them into the castle-yard tomorrow, and show them the bones and the skulls of those whom you have already put an end to. Make them believe, that before the end of the week, you will also tear them in pieces, as you have done to the others."*

So when the morning came, the Giant went to the Pilgrims and took them into the castle-yard, just as his wife had bidden him.

"These," he boasted, *"were once Pilgrims as you are. They trespassed on my grounds, just as you have done and when I saw fit, I tore them in pieces. In the same way, within ten days, I will do so to you! Now go down to your den again!"*

With that, he beat them all the way back to the den. Christian and Hopeful lay, therefore, all day in the same lamentable state.

Now night had come, and when Mrs. Diffidence and her husband, the Giant, went to bed, they began to renew their discourse about the prisoners. The old Giant wondered why he could neither, by his blows nor by his counsel, bring them to an end.

And with that his wife reasoned, *"I fear that they live in hope that someone will come to rescue them, or that they have picklocks with them, by which they hope to escape."*

"Do you think so, my dear?" responded the Giant, *"I will, therefore, search them in the morning."*

Now, about midnight, the Pilgrims began to pray and continued in prayer until almost the break of day. Then Christian, half-bewildered, broke out in this passionate speech: *"What a fool I have been, to thus lie in this stinking dungeon, when I could have been free! I have a key called Promise in my bosom, which I am persuaded will open any lock in Doubting Castle!"*

Hopeful replied, *"That is good news, my brother, pluck it out of your bosom, and try it!"*

Then Christian pulled it out of his bosom, and tried to unlock the dungeon door. As he turned the key, the bolt drew back and the door flew open! Christian and Hopeful quickly came out of the dungeon, and went to the outer door which led into the castle-yard. Using his key, Christian was able to open that door also.

Next they went to the iron gate of the castle, which also needed to be unlocked. Though this lock was very difficult to turn, yet the key finally opened it. Then they pushed the gate open to make a quick escape, but the gate, as it opened, made such a creaking, that it awakened Giant Despair. Hastily rising to pursue his prisoners, the Giant fell into one of his fits, and felt his limbs fail him, so that he was unable to go after them.

Then the Pilgrims found their way back to the King's highway and so were safe, being out of Giant Despair's jurisdiction.

Now, when they had gone back over the stile, they began to discuss what they should do to prevent others who would come after them, from falling into the hands of Giant Despair.

So they agreed to erect a pillar there and to engrave this warning upon it: *"Over this stile is the way to Doubting Castle, which is kept by Giant Despair, who despises the King of the Celestial Country, and seeks to destroy His holy Pilgrims!"*

This being done, they sang:

> *"Out of the way we went, and then we found*
> *What 'twas to tread upon forbidden ground;*
> *And let them who come after have a care,*
> *Lest heedlessness makes them, as we, to fare.*

Lest they for trespassing his prisoners are,
Whose castle's Doubting, and whose name's Despair."

Many, therefore, who later came to that place, read the warning and escaped the danger.

CHAPTER 22

THE DELECTABLE MOUNTAINS

Christian and Hopeful then went on until they came to the Delectable Mountains, which belong to the Lord of that hill of which we have spoken of before. So they went up to the mountains to behold the gardens, the orchards, the vineyards and the fountains of water. There they also washed themselves and freely drank and ate from the vineyards.

Now on the tops of these mountains, there were shepherds feeding their flocks while they stood by the highway side. The Pilgrims therefore went to them, and leaning upon their staffs, as is common with weary Pilgrims, when they stand to talk with any along the way, they asked, *"Whose Delectable Mountains are these? And whose are these sheep which feed upon them?"*

SHEPHERDS: *"These mountains are Immanuel's Land, and they are within sight of His City. The sheep are His also, for He laid down His life for them."*

CHRISTIAN: *"Is this the way to the Celestial City?"*

SHEPHERDS: *"Yes, this is the right way."*

CHRISTIAN: *"How far is it to the City?"*

SHEPHERDS: *"Too far for any, except for those who shall get there indeed."*

CHRISTIAN: *"Is the way safe or dangerous?"*

SHEPHERDS: *"The way is safe for those for whom it is meant to be safe. The righteous walk in it, but transgressors stumble in it."*

CHRISTIAN: *"Is there any relief in this place, for Pilgrims who are weary and faint?"*

SHEPHERDS: *"The Lord of these mountains has given us a charge to show hospitality to strangers, therefore the refreshment of the place is available for your welfare."*

I saw also in my dream, that when the Shepherds perceived that they were Pilgrims, they questioned them, *"Where did you come from? How did you get into the way? By what means have you persevered in the narrow way, for few of those who begin to come here, ever show their face on these mountains."* To all these questions, the Pilgrims answered as they had done previously.

When the Shepherds heard their answers, they were pleased and looked very lovingly upon them. They exclaimed, *"Welcome to the Delectable Mountains!"*

The Shepherds, whose names were Knowledge, Experience, Watchful, and Sincere, took them by the hand, brought them to their tents, and bid them to partake of a meal which had been prepared.

They said, moreover, *"We desire that you should stay here a while, to become acquainted with us and also to refresh yourselves with the good things of these Delectable Mountains."*

Then the Pilgrims told the Shepherds that they were content to stay. So they went to their rest that night, because it was very late.

Then I saw in my dream, that in the morning the Shepherds called Christian and Hopeful to walk with them upon the mountains. So they went forth with them, and walked a while, having a pleasant view on every side.

Then the Shepherds said to one another, *"Shall we show these Pilgrims some wonders?"*

When they concluded to do so, they first took them to the top of the Hill Error, which was very steep on the furthest side and bid the Pilgrims to look down to the bottom. So Christian and Hopeful looked down, and saw at the bottom, several men who had been dashed to pieces, having fallen from the top of the hill.

Then Christian asked, *"What does this mean?"*

The Shepherds responded, *"Have you not heard of those who erred by hearkening to Hymeneus and Philetus, as concerning the belief of the resurrection of the body?"*

"Yes," they replied.

Then the Shepherds explained, *"These are who you see dashed in pieces at the bottom of this mountain. They have continued to this day unburied, as you see, for an example to others to take heed not to come too near to the brink of Hill Error."*

Then I saw that the Shepherds brought them to the top of another mountain, named Caution and entreated them to look afar off. When they looked, they observed what they thought were several men walking up and down among the tombs that were there. They perceived that the men were blind, because they stumbled upon the tombstones, and could not find their way out from among them.

Then Christian questioned, *"What does this mean?"*

The Shepherds then explained, *"Did you not see that a little below these mountains, there was a stile which led into a meadow, on the left hand of the way?"*

"Yes," the Pilgrims replied.

The Shepherds then continued, *"From that stile leads a path which goes directly to Doubting Castle, which is kept by Giant Despair. These blind men among the tombs were once on pilgrimage, just as you are now. When they came to that stile, because the right way was rough, they chose to go out of it, and into that meadow. They were then captured by Giant Despair, and cast into Doubting Castle.*

"After they had been kept a while in the Giant's dungeon, he gouged out their eyes, and led them among those tombs, where he has left them to wander to this very day. So the saying of the wise man is fulfilled, 'Whoever strays out of the way of wisdom, shall remain in the congregation of the dead!'"

Then Christian and Hopeful looked upon one another with tears gushing out, yet they said nothing to the Shepherds.

Then I saw in my dream, that the Shepherds led them to another place, where there was a door in the side of a hill. They opened the door, and bid the Pilgrims to look in. Peering in, they saw that it was very dark and smoky. They also thought that they heard a rumbling noise as of fire, and a cry of some who were tormented, and that they smelled the scent of brimstone.

"What does this mean?" Christian inquired.

The Shepherds told them, *"This is a Byway to Hell, a way that hypocrites go. Namely, such as sell their birthright, with Esau. And such as sell their master, with Judas. And such as blaspheme the Gospel, with Alexander. And such as lie and deceive, with Ananias and his wife Sapphira."*

Then Hopeful questioned the Shepherds, *"I perceive that all of these once had a reputation as being Pilgrims, just as we do, had they not?"*

SHEPHERDS: *"Yes, and some held to it for a long time, too."*

HOPEFUL: *"How far they went on in pilgrimage, yet notwithstanding, they were thus miserably cast away!"*

SHEPHERDS: *"Some not so far as these mountains and some went further."*

Then the Pilgrims said to each another, *"We had need to cry to the Strong One for strength!"*

SHEPHERDS: *"Yes, and you will also have need to use that strength, when you have it."*

By this time the Pilgrims desired to resume their journey, and the Shepherds agreed. So they walked together towards the end of the mountains.

The Shepherds then said to each other, *"Let us here show the Pilgrims the gates of the Celestial City, if they have skill to look through our special telescope."*

The Pilgrims cordially agreed and were taken to the top of a high hill, called Clear, and were given the telescope. When they attempted to look, the remembrance of that last thing that the Shepherds had shown them, made their hands shake. With this impediment, they could not look steadily through the telescope. Yet they thought they saw something like the gate of the City, and also some of the glory of that place.

Then they went away, and sang this song:

> *"Thus, by the Shepherds, secrets are revealed,*
> *Which from all other men are kept concealed.*
> *Come to the Shepherds, then, if you would see,*
> *Things deep, things hid, and that mysterious be."*

When they were about to depart, one of the Shepherds gave them a note with directions for the way. Another warned them to beware of the Flatterer. The third bid them to take heed that they do not sleep upon the Enchanted Ground. And the fourth Shepherd bid them Godspeed.

So I awoke from my dream.

CHAPTER 23

IGNORANCE

Then I slept, and dreamed again. I saw the same two Pilgrims going down the mountains along the highway towards the Celestial City. Now, a little below these mountains, on the left hand, lies the country of Conceit. From this country a little crooked lane enters the narrow way in which the Pilgrims were walking. Here they met with a very boisterous lad named Ignorance, who came out of that country. So Christian asked him where he came from and where he was going.

IGNORANCE: *"Sir, I was born in the country which lies yonder, a little on the left hand and I am going to the Celestial City."*

CHRISTIAN: *"You may find some difficulty there. How do you suppose that you will enter the gate of the Celestial City?"*

IGNORANCE: *"Just as other good people do."*

CHRISTIAN: *"But what have you to show at that gate, which will allow you to enter there?"*

IGNORANCE: *"I know my Lord's will, and have lived a good life. I pay every man his due. I pray, fast, pay tithes, and give alms. Also, I have left my country for the very purpose of going there."*

CHRISTIAN: *"But you did not come in at the narrow-gate at the head of this way. You came into the way through that crooked lane. Therefore, I fear, however you may think of yourself, when the reckoning day shall come, that you will be charged with being a thief and a robber, rather than being admitted into the city."*

IGNORANCE: *"Gentlemen, I do not know you, for you are utter strangers to me. You be content to follow the religion of your country and I will follow the religion of mine. I trust that all will be well for each of us. And as for the narrow gate which you speak of, all the world knows that it is a great way off from our country. I do not think that any of my countrymen even know the way to it. Nor does it matter whether they do or not, since we have, as you see, a fine pleasant green lane, which comes down from our country into the way."*

When Christian saw that the man was wise in his own eyes, he whispered to Hopeful, *"There is more hope for a fool, than for him! Even as he walks along the road, the fool lacks sense and demonstrates how foolish he is. Shall we talk with him more, or leave him to think about what he has already heard, and then afterwards see if we can help him any further?"*

Then Hopeful answered,

"Let Ignorance a little while now muse,
On what is said, and let him not refuse
Good counsel to embrace, lest he remain,
Still ignorant of what's the chief gain.
God says, those who no understanding have,
Although He made them, them He will not save."

Hopeful further added, *"I do not think that it is good to tell him everything at once. Let us pass him by and talk with him later, as he is able to bear it."*

So the two Pilgrims went on, and Ignorance followed after them.

When they had traveled a little way, they entered into a

very dark lane, where they met a man whom seven devils had bound with seven strong cords, and were carrying him back to the door which they had seen on the side of the hill. Now good Christian began to tremble and so did his companion Hopeful! As the devils carried the man away, Christian looked to see if he knew him and he thought it might be Turn-away, who dwelt in the town of Apostasy. But he did not see his face perfectly, for the man hung his head like a thief who has been caught.

Once passed them, Hopeful looked at the man, and spotted a placard on his back with this inscription, *"Debauched professor, and damnable apostate!"*

Then Christian said to Hopeful, *"Now I remember what was told to me about something which happened to a good man named Little-faith who dwelt in the town of Sincere. As Little-faith entered this dark passage, there came down from Broad-way Gate, an alley called Dead Man's Lane, so called because of the many murders done there. This Little-faith, going on pilgrimage, just as we are, happened to sit down there, and fell asleep. Just at that time, three sturdy rogues, who were brothers, came down the lane from Broad-way Gate. Their names were Faint-heart, Mistrust, and Guilt. Spotting Little-faith asleep, they quickly ran up to him.*

"Now Little-faith was just awakening from his sleep, and was about to resume his journey. So the rogues came up to him, and with threatening language ordered him to stand still. At this, Little-faith turned as white as a sheet, and had neither power to fight nor flee.

"Then Faint-heart demanded, 'Hand over your purse!'

"But Little-faith did not do it, for he was reluctant to lose his money. Mistrust therefore ran up to him, and thrusting his hand into his pocket, pulled out a bag of silver.

"Then Little-faith cried out, 'Thieves! Thieves!'

"With that, Guilt, with the large club in his hand, struck Little-faith

on the head, knocking him flat to the ground! There he lay bleeding, as though he would bleed to death.

"All this while the thieves stood nearby. But hearing someone on the road, and fearing that it might be a man called Great-grace, who dwells in the city of Good-confidence, they fled and left Little-faith to fend for himself. Then, after a while, Little-faith revived, and getting up, attempted to continue on his way."

HOPEFUL: "Did they take all of Little-faith's money?"

CHRISTIAN: "No, they did not find the place where he kept his jewels, so those he still retained. But, as I was told, Little-faith was much afflicted by his loss, for the thieves got most of his spending-money. That which they did not get, were his jewels, and a little spare money, but these were scarcely enough to sustain him to his journey's end. Nay, if I am not misinformed, he was forced to beg as he went, just to keep himself alive, for he would not sell his jewels. But begging, and doing whatever he could, he traveled with a hungry belly the rest of the way."

HOPEFUL: "It is a wonder that they did not get his certificate from him, by which he would receive admittance at the Celestial Gate."

CHRISTIAN: "Yes, it is a wonder, though they did not get it through any cleverness on his part. For he, being bewildered by their coming upon him so quickly, had neither power nor skill to hide anything. So it was more by good Providence, than by any wise endeavor on his part, that they did not rob him of his certificate."

HOPEFUL: "But it must be a comfort to him, that they did not get his jewels."

CHRISTIAN: "It might have been great comfort to him, had he used his jewels as he should have. Those who told me the story, said that he made but little use of them because he was so discouraged from being robbed of his money. Indeed, he forgot about his jewels for a great part *of the rest of his journey. Whenever they came to his mind, and he began to be comforted with them, then fresh thoughts of his loss would again come upon him, and those thoughts would swallow up all comfort."*

HOPEFUL: *"Alas! poor man. This must have been a great grief to him."*

CHRISTIAN: *"Grief! Yes, a grief indeed. It would have been so to any of us, had we been robbed and wounded as he was and that in a strange place! It is a wonder that he did not die from grief, poor heart! I was told that he traveled almost all the rest of the way with nothing but doleful and bitter complaints, telling to all who overtook him, or whom he overtook as he journeyed, where and how he was robbed; who they were that did it; what he lost; how he was wounded; and that he hardly escaped with his life!"*

HOPEFUL: *"But it is a wonder that his necessity did not make him sell or pawn some of his jewels, that he might have something to sustain him along his journey."*

CHRISTIAN: *"You are talking childishly; for what could he pawn them for, or to whom could he sell them? In all that country where he was robbed, his jewels were not considered valuable; nor did he desire that kind of help which that country would offer. Besides, had his jewels been missing at the gate of the Celestial City, he knew that he would be excluded from an inheritance there and that would have been worse to him than the villainy of ten thousand thieves!"*

HOPEFUL: *"Why are you so short with me, my brother? Esau sold his birthright for a bowl of lentil stew and that birthright was his greatest jewel. If he could do this, then why might not Little-faith also?"*

CHRISTIAN: *"Esau indeed sold his birthright, and so do many others besides, but by doing so, they exclude themselves from their chief blessing, as despicable Esau did. There are differences between Esau and Little-faith, and also between their conditions. Esau's belly was his god, but not so with Little-faith. Esau's desire was his fleshly appetite, but not so with Little-faith. Besides, Esau could see no further than the fulfilling of his lusts, and said, 'Behold, I am at the point of death, what good can this birthright be to me?' But Little-faith, though it was his lot to have but a little faith, was by his little faith kept from Esau's base behavior. He prized his jewels, and would not consider selling them.*

"You nowhere read that Esau had faith, no, not so much as a little. As he was controlled by his fleshly appetites, and had no faith to resist, it is no wonder that he sold his birthright, and his soul and all, and that to the devil of Hell. Like a wild donkey in heat, when people like Esau have their minds set upon their lusts, they are determined to have them whatever the cost.

But Little-faith was of another temperament, his mind was on divine things; his desire was for things that were spiritual, and from above. Even if there had been any who would have bought his jewels, he had no desire to sell them, only to fill his mind with trifles. Would a man give a penny, to fill his belly with hay? Could you persuade the turtle-dove, to live upon carrion like the crow? Though faithless ones can, for carnal lusts, pawn or sell what they have, and themselves to boot, yet those who have faith, saving faith, though but a little of it, cannot do so. Here, therefore, my brother, is your mistake."

HOPEFUL: *"I acknowledge it, but yet your severe admonition almost made me angry."*

CHRISTIAN: *"If we only consider the matter under debate, then all shall be well between you and me."*

HOPEFUL: *"But, Christian, I am persuaded in my heart that these three rogues who attacked Little-faith were but a company of cowards, for they ran away merely at the sound of someone coming on the road. Why did Little-faith not have more courage? I think he might have withstood one skirmish and only have yielded when he could no longer resist them."*

CHRISTIAN: *"Though many have said that these three rouges are cowards, few have been willing to actually resist them. As for courage, Little-faith had none; and I perceive that you, my brother, if you had been the man concerned, you think that you could have withstood a skirmish before yielding. And since this is the height of your courage, now that they are at a distance from us, should they appear to you now as they did to him then, you might have second thoughts!*

"Consider again, they are but amateur thieves who serve under the king of the bottomless pit, whose voice is like that of a roaring lion, who will himself come to their aid, if need be.

"I myself have been assaulted just as Little-faith was and I found it to be a terrible thing! These three villains assailed me, and as a Christian, I began to resist them. But they called out and in came their evil master. I would, as the saying goes, have given my life for a penny, but as God would have it, I was clothed with armor. Yet, though I was so well arrayed, I found it hard work to stand firm and be courageous. No man can tell how strenuous that combat is, except he who has been in the battle himself."

HOPEFUL: *"Well, but they ran, you see, when they thought that Great-grace was coming."*

CHRISTIAN: *"True, they have often fled, both they and their master, when Great-grace has but appeared and no wonder, for he is the King's Champion. But I trust that you will see some difference between Little-faith and the King's Champion. All the King's subjects are not His champions, nor can they, when tried, do such feats of war as Great-grace. Is it reasonable to think that a little child could handle Goliath, as David did, or that there should be the strength of an ox, in a bird? Some are strong, some are weak; some have great faith, some have little faith. Little-faith was one of the weak and therefore he fared so poorly."*

HOPEFUL: *"I wish it had been Great-grace, for their sakes."*

CHRISTIAN: *"If it had been, he might have had his hands full; for I must tell you, that though Great-grace is excellent at his weapons, and has, and can, so long as he keeps them at sword's point, do well enough with them; yet, if Faint-heart, Mistrust, or Guilt get within his heart, they will be able to throw him down. And when a man is down, what can he do?*

"Whoever looks closely upon Great-grace's face, shall see those scars and cuts there, which demonstrates what I am saying. Yes, I once heard that he would say, when he was in combat, 'We despaired even of life!'

"How these sturdy rogues and their fellows made David groan and mourn! Yes, Heman and Hezekiah also, though champions in their day, were assaulted by these three rogues. Yet, notwithstanding, they had their coats soiled and torn by them. Peter also, whom some say that he is the prince of the apostles, thought that he could stand fast. But these rogues so handled him, that they even made him afraid of a poor maiden.

"Besides, their evil king is at their beck and call. When they whistle for him, he is never out of hearing. And if at any time they are being defeated, he will come in to help them. He esteems iron as straw and brass as rotten wood. The arrow cannot make him flee and he turns sling stones into chaff. He counts darts as stubble and he laughs at the shaking of a spear! What can a Pilgrim do in this case?

"But for such footmen as you and I are, let us never desire to meet with an enemy. Nor let us boast as if we could do better, when we hear of others who have been foiled; nor let us be proud of our own strength, for such overconfident fellows are commonly overcome when tried. Witness Peter, of whom I just mentioned. He would boast, yes, his vain mind prompted him to say that though all denied his Master, that he never would. But who has ever been so foiled by these villains, as Peter?

"When, therefore, we hear that such robberies are done on the King's highway, there are two things that we should do:

"First, to go out with our armor on and to be sure to take our shield with us. It is for lack of this, that many Pilgrims are foiled. Only the shield of faith can quench the fiery darts of the wicked one. If that is lacking, the wicked one does not fear us at all.

"Secondly, it is good, also, that we ask the King for a guide as we journey, yes, that He Himself would go with us. This made David rejoice when in the Valley of the Shadow of Death and Moses would rather die where he stood, rather than to go one step without God. O my brother, if He will but go with us, then we will not be afraid of tens of thousands who set themselves against us. But, without Him, we will only stumble along, or lie among the dead.

"Previously I myself have been in the fray and through the mercy of our good Master, I am still alive. Yet I cannot boast of having any courage. I would be glad to meet with no further attacks, though, I fear, we have not gotten beyond all danger. However, since the lion and the bear have not as yet devoured us, I trust God will also deliver us from the next uncircumcised Philistine."

Then Christian sang:

"Poor Little-faith has been among the thieves,
Was robbed, remember this; whosoever believes
And gets more faith, shall then a victor be
Over ten thousand, otherwise not even three."

CHAPTER 24

THE FLATTERER

So the Pilgrims went on, and Ignorance followed. They came to a path which seemed to go as straight as the way which they were on and hence they did not know which of the two to take, for both seemed straight before them. Therefore, they stood still to consider.

As they were thinking about the way, behold a man clothed with a very light robe, came to them, and asked them why they were standing there. They answered that they were going to the Celestial City, but did not know which of these ways to take.

"Follow me," the man said, *"I am going there also."*

So they followed him into the adjoining way, which slowly by degrees turned them away from the Celestial City, so that, in a little time, their faces were completely turned away from it; yet they continued to follow him. By and by, before they were aware, he led them into a net, in which they were both so entangled, that they did not know what to do. With that, the white robe fell off the man's back. Then they saw where they were. There they lay crying for some time, for they could not extricate themselves from the net.

Then Christian said to his fellow, *"Now I see my error. Did not the Shepherds bid us to beware of the Flatterer? As is the saying of the wise man, so we have found it this day: 'Whoever flatters his neighbor, is spreading a net for his feet!'"*

HOPEFUL: *"They also gave us a note with directions so that we could surely find the way, but we forgot to read it, and have wandered into the paths of the destroyer. Here David was wiser than we; for he said, 'By the word of Your lips, I have kept myself from the paths of the destroyer.'"*

Thus they lay in the net, bewailing themselves. At last they sighted a Shining One coming towards them, with a whip of small cords in his hand. When he arrived at the place where they were, he asked them where they came from, and what they were doing there.

They told him that they were poor Pilgrims going to the Celestial City, but were led out of their way by a man who was clothed in white, who bid them to follow him, for he was going there also.

Then the Shining One replied, *"That was the Flatterer! He is a false apostle, who transforms himself into an angel of light."*

So he cut the net, and freed the Pilgrims. Then he said to them, *"Follow me, so that I may place you in the right path again."*

So he led them back to the way which they had left to follow the Flatterer. Then he asked them, *"Where did you stay last night?"*

They answered, *"With the Shepherds, upon the Delectable Mountains."*

He then asked if the Shepherds had given them a note with directions for the way.

"Yes," they responded.

"Did you not read your note?" he questioned.

"No," they replied.

"And why not?" He asked them.

They answered that they had forgotten.

He asked, moreover, if the Shepherds told them to beware of the Flatterer.

"Yes," they explained, *"but we did not imagine that he was this fine-spoken man."*

Then I saw in my dream, that he commanded the Pilgrims to lie down. Having done this, he grievously chastised them, to teach them the good way in which they should walk. As he chastised them, he declared, *"As many as I love, I rebuke and chasten. Be zealous, therefore, and repent."*

This done, he bid them to go on their way, and to pay close attention to the other directions which the Shepherds had given them. So they thanked him for all his kindness, and went carefully along the right way, singing:

> *"Come here, you who walk along the way;*
> *See how Pilgrims fare, who go astray!*
> *They are catched in an entangling net,*
> *Cause they good counsel, did forget.*
>
> *'Tis true, they were rescued, but yet you see,*
> *They're scourged to boot, let this your caution be."*

CHAPTER 25

ATHEIST

Now, after a while, they perceived afar off, one coming softly along the highway to meet them.

Then Christian said to his fellow, *"Yonder is a man with his back toward the Celestial City, and he is coming to meet us."*

HOPEFUL: *"I see him. Let us be careful now, lest he should prove to be a flatterer also."*

So the man drew nearer and nearer, and at last came up to them. His name was Atheist, and he asked them where they were going.

CHRISTIAN: *"We are going to the Celestial City."*

Then Atheist burst into laughter.

CHRISTIAN: *"What is the meaning of your laughter?"*

ATHEIST: *"I laugh because I see what ignorant people you are, to take so tedious a journey, and yet are likely to gain nothing for your travel but pains."*

CHRISTIAN: *"Why do you think we shall not be received?"*

ATHEIST: *"Received! There is no such place as you dream of in all this world!"*

CHRISTIAN: *"That is true, but there is in the world to come."*

ATHEIST: *"When I was at home in my own country, I heard of that place which you speak of. So I went out to find it and have been seeking this City for these past twenty years; but I have not found it in all this time!"*

CHRISTIAN: *"We have both heard and believe that there is such a place to be found!"*

ATHEIST: *"Had not I, when at home, also believed, I would not have come thus far to seek it. If there had been such a place, I would have surely found it by now, for I have gone much further than you. So not finding it, I am going back home again, and will seek the pleasures which I had then cast away, for the vain hope of a world to come."*

Then Christian said to Hopeful, *"Do you think that what this man has said is true?"*

HOPEFUL: *"Take heed, he is one of the flatterers! Remember what it has cost us once already for our hearkening to such a fellow. What! No Celestial City? Did we not see, from the Delectable Mountains, the gate of the City? Also, we are now to walk by faith. Let us go on, lest the man with the whip overtake us again.*

"You should have taught me that lesson, which I will now remind you of: 'Do not listen to any advice which would lead you to stray from the words of knowledge.' I say, my brother, do not listen to him, but let us believe to the saving of our souls!"

CHRISTIAN: *"My brother, I did not ask the question of you, because I doubted the truth myself, but to test you, and to hear your heartfelt response. As for this man, I know that he is blinded by the god of this world. Let us go on, knowing that we believe the truth, and that no lie is of the truth."*

HOPEFUL: *"Now I rejoice in the hope of the glory of God!"*

So they turned away from the man and he, laughing at them, went on his way back home.

CHAPTER 26

THE ENCHANTED GROUND

Then I saw in my dream, that they went on until they came to a certain country, whose air naturally tended to make travelers drowsy.

So Hopeful began to be very dull and sleepy, and said to Christian, *"I am starting to grow so drowsy that I can scarcely hold my eyes open. Let us lay down here, and take a nap."*

CHRISTIAN: *"By no means, lest by sleeping, we never wake up again!"*

HOPEFUL: *"Why, my brother? Sleep is sweet to the laboring man, we may be refreshed if we take a nap."*

CHRISTIAN: *"Do you not remember that one of the Shepherds warned us to beware of the Enchanted Ground? Therefore let us not sleep, as others do, but let us keep awake and watch."*

HOPEFUL: *"I acknowledge my fault. Had I been here alone, I would have slept and been in danger of death. I see that what the wise man said is true: 'Two are better than one.' Your company been a mercy to me and you shall have a good reward for your labor."*

"Now then," Christian said, *"to prevent drowsiness in this place, let us have a wholesome discussion."*

"With all my heart," said Hopeful.

CHRISTIAN: *"Where shall we begin?"*

HOPEFUL: *"Where God began with us. Please start."*

CHRISTIAN: *"First I will sing this song to you:*

When saints do sleepy grow, let them come hither,
And hear how these two Pilgrims talk together.
Yes, let them learn of them, in any wise,
Thus to keep open their drowsy, slumbering eyes.
Saints' fellowship, if it be managed well,
Keeps them awake, and that in spite of Hell."

Then Christian began, *"I will ask you a question. How did you come at first, to think of going on this pilgrimage?"*

HOPEFUL: *"Do you mean, how did I first come to look after the good of my soul?"*

CHRISTIAN: *"Yes, that is my meaning."*

HOPEFUL: *"I continued a great while in the delight of those vain things which were seen and sold at our fair. These things I now believe, had I continued in them still, would have drowned me in perdition and destruction!"*

CHRISTIAN: *"What things were they?"*

HOPEFUL: *"All the treasures and riches of the world. I also delighted much in carousing, drinking, swearing, lying, impurity, Sabbath-breaking, and what not, all of which lead to the destruction of the soul. But I found at last, by hearing and considering divine things, which I heard from you and beloved Faithful, (who was put to death for his faith and holy living in Vanity Fair) that the end of these things is death! And that for these things, the wrath of God comes upon the children of disobedience!"*

CHRISTIAN: *"Did you immediately fall under the power of this conviction?"*

HOPEFUL: *"No, I was not initially willing to know the evil of sin, nor the damnation which follows the commission of sin. Rather, when my mind at first began to be shaken with the Word, I endeavored to shut my eyes against its light."*

CHRISTIAN: *"But what was the cause for your resistence to the first workings of God's blessed Spirit upon you?"*

HOPEFUL: *"There were several causes:*

"First, I was ignorant that this was the work of God upon me. I never thought that God begins the conversion of a sinner through convictions of sin.

"Secondly, sin was yet very sweet to my flesh and I was reluctant to leave it.

"Thirdly, I could not tell how to part with my old companions, their presence and actions were so desirable to me.

"Finally, my convictions of sin were so troublesome and heart-affrighting, that I could not endure the thought of them in my heart."

CHRISTIAN: *"Then, as it seems, sometimes you got rid of your convictions of sin?"*

HOPEFUL: *"Yes, truly, but they would come into my mind again, and then I would be as bad, nay, worse than I was before."*

CHRISTIAN: *"Why, what was it that brought your sins to mind again?"*

HOPEFUL: *"Many things, such as,*

If I did but meet a godly man in the streets; or,

If I heard anyone read in the Bible; or,

If my head began to ache; or,

If I was told that some of my neighbors were sick; or,

If I heard the death-bell toll for someone who had died; or,

If I thought of dying myself; or,

If I heard that another had died by sudden death.

But especially, when I thought of myself, that I must quickly come to judgment!"

CHRISTIAN: *"And could you easily at any time, get off the guilt of sin, when, by any of these ways, conviction came upon you?"*

HOPEFUL: *"No, not I, for then they got a tighter hold on my conscience. And then, if I did but think of going back to sin, though my mind was turned against it, it would be double torment to me."*

CHRISTIAN: *"And what did you do then?"*

HOPEFUL: *"I reckoned that I must endeavor to mend my life, for I thought that otherwise, I was sure to be damned."*

CHRISTIAN: *"And did you ever attempt to mend your life?"*

HOPEFUL: *"Yes, and I fled not only from my sins, but from sinful company too. I also began religious duties, such as prayer, reading, weeping for sin, speaking truth to my neighbors, and so forth. These things I did, along with many others, too many to recount."*

CHRISTIAN: *"And did you think yourself well then?"*

HOPEFUL: *"Yes, for a while, but eventually my troubling convictions came tumbling upon me again, in spite of all my reformations."*

CHRISTIAN: *"How so, since you were now reformed?"*

HOPEFUL: *"There were several things which brought these convictions upon me, especially such sayings as these: 'All our righteousnesses are as filthy rags.' 'By the works of the law shall no flesh be justified.' 'When we have done everything we should, we are unworthy servants, doing but our duty', along with many more similar sayings. Hence I began to reason thus with myself: If ALL my righteousnesses are filthy rags and if, by the deeds of the law, NO man can be justified and if, when we have done ALL our duty, we are yet unprofitable servants, then it is but folly to think of gaining Heaven by keeping the law.*

"I further thought thus: If a man runs a hundred dollars into debt to the shopkeeper, and from then on, he pays for everything that he purchases; yet, if his old debt still remains unpaid in the ledger book, the shopkeeper will sue him for that, and cast him into prison until he shall pay the full debt."

CHRISTIAN: *"So how did you apply this to yourself?"*

HOPEFUL: *"Why, I thought thus with myself: I have, by my sins, accumulated a great debt in God's Book and that my now reforming will not pay off that debt. Therefore even with all my present amendments, I would not be freed from that damnation which my former transgressions still deserved."*

CHRISTIAN: *"A very good application, but please go on."*

HOPEFUL: *"Another thing which troubled me, even since my recent amendments, is that if I look closely into the best of whatever I do, I still see sin, new sin, mixing itself with my best deeds. So I am forced to conclude, that notwithstanding my former good opinion of myself and my duties, I have committed enough sin in one duty to send me to Hell, even if my former life had been faultless!"*

CHRISTIAN: *"And what did you do then?"*

HOPEFUL: *"Do! I did not know what to do, until I shared my thoughts with Faithful, for we were well acquainted. He told me that unless I could obtain the righteousness of a Man who never had sinned, that neither my own, nor all the righteousness of the world, could save me."*

CHRISTIAN: *"And did you think he spoke the truth?"*

HOPEFUL: *"Had he told me this while I was yet pleased and satisfied with my own amendments, I would have called him a fool for his coun-*

sel. But now, since I see my own error, and the sin which cleaves to even my best performances, I was forced to embrace his opinion."

CHRISTIAN: *"But did you think, when at first he suggested it to you, that there was such a Man to be found, of whom it might justly be said, that He never committed any sin?"*

HOPEFUL: *"I must confess that his words did sound strange at first, but after a little more conversation with him, I was fully convinced."*

CHRISTIAN: *"And did you ask Faithful who this Man was and how you must be justified by Him?"*

HOPEFUL: *"Yes, and he told me it was the Lord Jesus, who dwells on the right hand of the Most High God. And thus he said that I must be justified by Him, even by trusting in what He Himself has done during His earthly life and what He suffered when He hung on the tree.*

"I asked him further, how that Man's righteousness could be effectual to justify another before God? And he told me that He was the mighty God, and that both His life and His death, was not for Himself, but for me, to whom the worthiness of His doings would be imputed, if I believed on Him."

CHRISTIAN: *"And what did you do then?"*

HOPEFUL: *"I made objections against my believing, for I thought that He was not willing to save me."*

CHRISTIAN: *"And what did Faithful say to you then?"*

HOPEFUL: *"He bid me to go to Him and see. And I told him that this would be presumption. But he said, 'Not so, for I was invited to come.' Then he gave me a Book of Jesus, in His own words, to encourage me to come the more freely. He also said, concerning that Book, that its every jot and tittle stood firmer than Heaven and earth.*

"Then I asked Faithful what I must do when I go to Him. He told me

that I must entreat the Father upon my knees and with all my heart and soul, to reveal the Lord Jesus to me.

"*Then I asked him further, how I must make my petition to Him? And he said, 'Go, and you shall find Him upon a mercy-seat, where He sits all the year long, to give pardon and forgiveness to those who come.'*

"*I told him that I did not know what to say when I go. And he bid me to say something to this effect: 'God be merciful to me a sinner and make me to know and believe in Jesus Christ. For I see that if He had not provided His perfect righteousness, or if I have not faith in His righteousness, then I am utterly cast away. Lord, I have heard that You are a merciful God, and have ordained that Your Son Jesus Christ should be the Savior of the world; and moreover, that you are willing to bestow Him upon such a poor sinner as I am and I am a poor sinner indeed. Lord, be pleased to magnify Your grace in the salvation of my soul, through Your Son Jesus Christ. Amen.'*"

CHRISTIAN: "*And did you do as you were bidden?*"

HOPEFUL: "*Yes, over, and over, and over.*"

CHRISTIAN: "*And did the Father reveal His Son to you?*"

HOPEFUL: "*Not at the first, nor the second, nor the third, nor the fourth, nor the fifth, no, not even at the sixth time.*"

CHRISTIAN: "*What did you do then?*"

HOPEFUL: "*What! Why I could not tell what to do!*"

CHRISTIAN: "*Did you ever consider giving up praying?*"

HOPEFUL: "*Yes, a hundred times, twice over!*"

CHRISTIAN: "*And what was the reason why you did not?*"

HOPEFUL: "*I believed that what Faithful told me was true, namely, that without the righteousness of Christ, all the world could not save me. Therefore, I thought that if I cease praying, I would die and I dare not die, except at the throne of grace. Then this thought came into my mind, 'Though it seems slow in coming, wait patiently, for it will surely take place.' So I continued praying until the Father revealed His Son to me."*

CHRISTIAN: *"And how was He revealed unto you?"*

HOPEFUL: *"I did not see Him with my bodily eyes, but with the eyes of my understanding. It happened in this way: One day I was very sad, perhaps sadder than at any other time in my life. This sadness sprang from a fresh sight of the immensity and vileness of my sins. As I was then expecting nothing but Hell and the everlasting damnation of my soul, suddenly I thought I saw the Lord Jesus look down from Heaven upon me, and say, 'Believe on the Lord Jesus Christ and you shall be saved.'*

"But I replied, 'Lord, I am a dreadful sinner, a very dreadful sinner.'

"And He answered, 'My grace is sufficient for you.'

"Then I said, 'but, Lord, what is believing?'

"And then I saw from that saying, 'He who comes to Me shall never hunger, and he who believes on Me shall never thirst', that believing and coming were one and the same; and that he who came, that is, he who ran out in his heart and affections after salvation by Christ, he indeed believed in Christ.

"Then the water stood in my eyes, and I asked further: 'But Lord, may such a vile sinner as I am, indeed be accepted by You, and be saved by You?'

"And I heard Him say, 'Whoever comes to Me, I will never cast out.'

"Then I said, 'But how Lord, in my coming to You, must I properly think of You, that my faith may be rightly placed upon You?'

"And He said, 'Christ Jesus came into the world to save sinners.' 'He is

the end of the law for righteousness to everyone who believes.' 'He died for our sins, and rose again for our justification.' 'He loved us, and washed us from our sins in His own blood.' 'He is the mediator between God and men.' 'He ever lives to make intercession for us.'

"From all of this, I gathered that I must look for righteousness in His person, and for atonement for my sins by His blood. Also, that what He did in obedience to His Father's law, and in submitting to its penalty, was not for Himself, but for the one who will accept it for his salvation, and be thankful.

"And now my heart was full of joy, my eyes were full of tears, and my affections were running over, with love to the name, ways and people of Jesus Christ."

CHRISTIAN: "This was a revelation of Christ to your soul indeed! But tell me particularly, what effect this encounter had upon your spirit."

HOPEFUL: "First, it made me see that all the world, notwithstanding all its boasted righteousness, is in a state of condemnation.

"Secondly, it made me see that God the Father is both just and the Justifier of the one who believes in Jesus.

"Thirdly, it made me greatly ashamed of the vileness of my former life, and confounded me with the sense of my own ignorance; for I never had a thought in my heart before now, that so showed me the beauty of Jesus Christ.

"Lastly, it made me love a holy life, and long to do something for the honor and glory of the name of the Lord Jesus. Yes, I thought that had I now a thousand gallons of blood in my body, I could spill it all for the sake of the Lord Jesus."

CHAPTER 27

IGNORANCE REJOINS THE PILGRIMS

Then I saw in my dream, that Hopeful looked back and saw Ignorance, whom they had left behind, following after them.

"Look," he said to Christian, *"Ignorance is still lagging behind us!"*

CHRISTIAN: *"Yes, yes, I see him, he does not care for our company."*

HOPEFUL: *"It would not have hurt him, had he stayed with us thus far."*

CHRISTIAN: *"That is true, but I guarantee that he thinks otherwise."*

HOPEFUL: *"I agree, however, let us wait for him."*

So they did.

Then Christian called to Ignorance, *"Come join us, why do you stay so far behind?"*

IGNORANCE: *"It pleases me to walk alone, rather than in company, unless of course, the company suits me better."*

Then Christian whispered to Hopeful, *"Did I not tell you that he did not care for our company?"*

Then, calling out to Ignorance, Christian said, *"Come up, and let us talk away the time in this solitary place. Say, how are you doing? How does it now stand between God and your soul?"*

IGNORANCE: *"I hope well, for I am always full of good notions that come into my mind, to comfort me as I walk."*

CHRISTIAN: *"What good notions? Please tell us."*

IGNORANCE: *"Why, I think of God and Heaven."*

CHRISTIAN: *"So do the devils and damned souls."*

IGNORANCE: *"But I think of them and desire them."*

CHRISTIAN: *"So do many who are never likely to get to Heaven. The soul of the sluggard desires and gets nothing!"*

IGNORANCE: *"But I think of God and Heaven and leave all for them."*

CHRISTIAN: *"That I doubt, for leaving all is a hard matter, yes, a harder matter than many are aware of. But why do you think that you have left all for God and Heaven?"*

IGNORANCE: *"Because my heart tells me so."*

CHRISTIAN: *"But the wise man says, 'He who trusts in his own heart is a fool.'"*

IGNORANCE: *"That was spoken of an evil heart, but mine is a good one."*

CHRISTIAN: *"But how do you prove that?"*

IGNORANCE: *"It comforts me in hopes of Heaven."*

CHRISTIAN: *"That may be through your heart's deceitfulness; for a man's heart may minister comfort to him in the hope of Heaven and yet be a false hope."*

IGNORANCE: *"But my heart and my life agree together and therefore my hope is well grounded."*

CHRISTIAN: *"Who told you that your heart and life agree together?"*

IGNORANCE: *"My heart tells me so."*

CHRISTIAN: *"Your heart tells you so! Except the Word of God bears witness in this matter, any other testimony is of no value!"*

IGNORANCE: *"But is it not a good heart, which has good thoughts? And is it not a good life, which is according to God's commandments?"*

CHRISTIAN: *"Yes, that is a good heart, which has good thoughts; and that is a good life, which is according to God's commandments. But it is one thing, indeed, to have a good heart and life and it is another thing only to think so."*

IGNORANCE: *"Tell me please, what you think are good thoughts, and a life according to God's commandments?"*

CHRISTIAN: *"There are good thoughts of many kinds, some respecting ourselves, some of God, some of Christ, and some of other things."*

IGNORANCE: *"What are good thoughts respecting ourselves?"*

CHRISTIAN: *"Such as agree with the Word of God."*

IGNORANCE: *"When do our thoughts of ourselves agree with the Word of God?"*

CHRISTIAN: *"When we pass the same judgment upon ourselves, which the Word passes. To explain myself, the Word of God says of people in their natural condition, 'There are none righteous, there are none who do good.' It says also, that 'every imagination of the heart of man is only evil, and that continually.' And again, 'The imagination of man's heart is evil from his youth.' Now then, when we think thus of ourselves, then our thoughts are good ones, because they are according to the Word of God."*

IGNORANCE: *"I will never believe that my heart is that bad!"*

CHRISTIAN: *"Therefore you never had one good thought concerning yourself in all of your life! But let me go on. As the Word passes a judg-*

ment upon our heart, so it passes a judgment upon our ways. When our thoughts concerning our hearts and our ways agree with the judgment which the Word gives of both, then are both good, because they are in agreement with the Word of God."

IGNORANCE: *"Explain what you mean by this."*

CHRISTIAN: *"Why, the Word of God says that man's ways are crooked and perverse and not good. It says that no one seeks God, but all have turned away from Him. Now, when a man sincerely thinks thus of his ways, and with heart humiliation, then his thoughts now agree with the judgment of the Word of God."*

IGNORANCE: *"Further, what are good thoughts concerning God?"*

CHRISTIAN: *"Just as I have said concerning ourselves, when our thoughts of God agree with what the Word says of Him. That is, when we think of His being and attributes just as the Word teaches, of which I cannot presently discourse at length.*

"To speak of Him with reference to ourselves, we have right thoughts of God, when we understand that He knows us better than we know ourselves, and can see sin in us when and where we can see no sin in ourselves. Also when we realize that He knows our inmost thoughts and that our heart, with all its depths, is always open before His eyes. Also, when we think that all our righteousness is a stench in His nostrils and that, therefore, He cannot endure to have us stand before Him in any self-confidence, even in all our best duties."

IGNORANCE: *"Do you think that I am such a fool as to imagine that God can see no further than I can, or, that I would come to God in the best of my duties?"*

CHRISTIAN: *"Well, what do you think concerning this matter?"*

IGNORANCE: *"Why, to be brief, I think I must believe in Christ for justification."*

CHRISTIAN: *"How can you believe in Christ, when you do not see your need of Him? You neither see your original nor actual sins! You have such a high opinion of yourself, and of what you do, so that you never see the necessity of Christ's personal righteousness to justify you before God. How, then, can you say that you believe in Christ?"*

IGNORANCE: *"My beliefs are fine, in spite of all that you have just said."*

CHRISTIAN: *"What exactly then, do you believe?"*

IGNORANCE: *"I believe that Christ died for sinners and that I shall be justified before God from the curse, through His gracious acceptance of my obedience to His law. To state it another way, Christ makes my religious duties acceptable to His Father, by virtue of His merits and so I shall be justified."*

CHRISTIAN: *"Let me give an answer to your beliefs on this issue.*

"First, you believe with an imaginary faith, for this kind of faith is nowhere described in the Word.

"Secondly, you believe with a false faith, because you trust that you are justified by your own righteousness, rather than the righteousness of Christ.

"Thirdly, your beliefs make Christ a justifier of your actions, but not of your person. You think that your person is justified for your action's sake, which is false.

"Therefore, your faith is deceitful, even such as will leave you under divine wrath, in the day of Almighty God's judgment. For true justifying faith causes the soul, being sensible of its lost condition by the law, to flee for refuge unto Christ's righteousness. It is not that Christ graciously makes a person's obedience acceptable to God, but true faith accepts Christ's righteousness by His personal obedience to the law, in doing and suffering for us what that law required at our hands. The soul, thus

covered in Christ's righteousness and presented as spotless before God, is accepted by God and acquitted from condemnation."

IGNORANCE: *"What! Would you have us trust to only what Christ, in His own person, has done for us? This belief would loosen the reins of our lusts, and allow us to live any sinful way we desire. For what would it matter how we live, if we believe that we are justified by Christ's personal righteousness alone?"*

CHRISTIAN: *"Ignorance is your name and as your name is, so you are! Your answer demonstrates what I say. You are ignorant of what justifying righteousness is and just as ignorant how to secure your soul from the dreadful wrath of God, through Christ's righteousness alone. Yes, you are also ignorant of the true effects of saving faith, such as, to submit the heart to God, to love His Name, His Word, His ways and His people and not as you ignorantly imagine."*

Hopeful then joined in and asked, *"Ignorance, has God ever revealed Christ to your heart?"*

IGNORANCE: *"What! You are a man for revelations! I think that what both of you, and all the rest of your kind say, is but the fruit of your disordered brains!"*

HOPEFUL: *"Why, Sir! Christ is so hidden from the natural understanding of men, that He cannot be savingly known, unless God the Father reveals Him to them."*

IGNORANCE: *"That is your belief, but not mine! My beliefs are as good as yours, though I do not have so many foolish notions in my head as you do."*

CHRISTIAN: *"Allow me to put in a word. You ought not to speak of this matter so lightly. I will boldly affirm, even as my good companion has done, that no man can know Jesus Christ but by the revelation of the Father.*

"Also, that faith by which a soul truly lays hold upon Christ, must be wrought by the exceeding greatness of God's mighty power. Poor Ignorance, I perceive that you are ignorant of the working of this faith in your own soul. Be awakened then, see your own wretchedness and flee to the Lord Jesus! By His divine righteousness alone, can you be delivered from condemnation."

IGNORANCE: *"You go too fast, I cannot keep pace with you. Go ahead of me, I must stay behind for a while."*

Then they said,

"Well, Ignorance, will you yet foolish be,
To slight good counsel, ten times given thee?

And if you yet refuse it, you shall know,
Before long, the evil of your doing so.

Remember, man, in time, bow, do not fear,
Good counsel taken well, saves, therefore hear.

But if you yet shall slight it, you will be
The loser (Ignorance) I'll warrant thee."

Christian then addressed Hopeful: *"Come, my good fellow, I see that you and I must walk by ourselves again."*

So I saw in my dream that they went on quickly, while Ignorance lagged behind.

Then Christian said to his companion, *"I feel much pity for this poor man, it will certainly go badly with him at the last."*

HOPEFUL: *"Alas! There are many in our town in his condition, whole families, yes, whole streets, and some claiming to be Pilgrims also. If there are so many in our parts, how many, do you think, must there be in the place where Ignorance was born?"*

CHRISTIAN: *"Indeed the Word says, 'He has blinded their eyes and hardened their hearts, lest they see with their eyes, and understand with their hearts, and turn and I would heal them.' But now that we are by ourselves, what do you think of such men as Ignorance? Do you think that they ever have real convictions of sin and subsequent fears that their state is dangerous?"*

HOPEFUL: *"Nay, I think that you should answer that question yourself, for you are older in experience."*

CHRISTIAN: *"Then, I think that they may sometimes have convictions of sin; but being naturally ignorant, they do not understand that such convictions tend to their good. Therefore they desperately seek to stifle them, and presumptuously continue to flatter themselves in the way of their own hearts."*

HOPEFUL: *"I do believe, as you say, that fear tends much to men's good, to set them right at their beginning to go on pilgrimage."*

CHRISTIAN: *"Without doubt it does, if it is right fear; for so says the Word, 'The fear of the Lord is the beginning of wisdom.'"*

HOPEFUL: *"How would you describe the right fear?"*

CHRISTIAN: *"True or right fear is manifested by three things:*

"First. By its rise, it is caused by saving convictions for sin.

"Second. It drives the soul to lay fast hold on Christ for salvation.

"Third. It begets and continues in the soul a great reverence of God, His Word, and His ways, keeping the soul tender, and making it afraid to turn from them, to the right hand or to the left, to anything that may dishonor God, break its peace, grieve the Spirit, or cause the enemy to speak reproachfully."

HOPEFUL: *"Well said! I believe you have explained the truth. Have we now almost gotten past the Enchanted Ground?"*

CHRISTIAN: *"Why, are you weary of this discourse?"*

HOPEFUL: *"No, truly, I would only like to know where we are."*

CHRISTIAN: *"We have less than two miles further to go. So let us return to our discussion. Now the ignorant do not understand that such convictions which tend to put them in fear, are for their good and therefore they seek to stifle them."*

HOPEFUL: *"How do they seek to stifle them?"*

So Christian explained,

"First, they think that those fears are wrought by the devil (though they are actually wrought by God); and, thinking so, they resist them as things which directly tend to their overthrow.

"Secondly, they also think that these fears tend to the destruction of their faith, when, alas for them, poor men that they are, they have no faith at all! So therefore they harden their hearts against them.

"Thirdly, they presume that they ought not to fear. Therefore, despite their fears, they increasingly become more presumptuous and self-confident.

"Finally, they see that those fears tend to take away their pathetic former self-righteousness, and therefore they resist them with all their might."

HOPEFUL: *"I know something of this myself, for, before I truly knew myself, it was the same with me."*

CHRISTIAN: *"Well, let us now leave our neighbor Ignorance to himself, and talk about another profitable question."*

HOPEFUL: *"With all my heart and you shall begin."*

CHRISTIAN: *"Well then, did you know, about ten years ago, one named Temporary in your parts, who was then a prominent man in religion?"*

HOPEFUL: *"Know him! Yes, he dwelt in Graceless, a town about two* miles away from Honesty, and he lived next door to a person named Turnback."

CHRISTIAN: *"Yes, and he actually dwelt under the same roof with Turnback. Well, that man was once much awakened, I believe that he then had some sight of his sins, and of the wages which were due for them."*

HOPEFUL: *"I agree, for my house, being less than three miles from his, he would often visit me with many tears. Truly, I pitied the man, and had some hope for him. But, as you know, not everyone who cries, 'Lord, Lord!' is saved."*

CHRISTIAN: *"He once told me that he was resolved to go on pilgrimage, just as we are now doing. But all of a sudden he grew acquainted with one named Save-self and then he became as a stranger to me."*

HOPEFUL: *"Now, since we are talking about him, let us investigate into the reason of his sudden backsliding, and others like him."*

CHRISTIAN: *"This may be very profitable, so please begin."*

HOPEFUL: *"Well then, in my judgment there are four reasons for backsliding:*

"First, though the consciences of such men are awakened, yet their minds are not changed. Therefore, when the power of guilt wears off, then that which caused them to become religious ceases, and they naturally turn to their own sinful course again. We see this illustrated in how a sick dog vomits what he has eaten, because it troubles his stomach. When his sickness is over, and his stomach is eased, the desire for what he has vomited returns and he licks it all up. And so that which is written is true, 'The dog returns to its own vomit!'

"They initially are eager for Heaven, but only out of the fear of the torments of Hell. But when their sense of Hell, and their fears of damnation chill and cool, so their desires for Heaven and salvation cool

also. It then comes to pass, that when their guilt and fear is gone, their desires for Heaven and its happiness die, and they return to their sinful course again.

"Another reason for backsliding, is that they have slavish fears which overmaster them. I speak now of the fears that they have of men, for 'the fear of man brings a snare.' Though they seem to be eager for Heaven, so long as the flames of Hell are about their ears, yet, when that terror diminishes, they begin to have second thoughts. They then think that it is wise not to run the hazard of losing all, or, at least, of bringing themselves into unavoidable and unnecessary troubles and so they return to their worldly ways again.

"Another stumbling-block which lies in their way, is the shame which attends religion. They are proud and haughty and religion is base and contemptible in their eyes. Therefore, when they have lost their sense of Hell and the wrath to come, they return again to their former sinful course.

"And finally, the feelings of guilt, and meditation on terrifying things, are grievous to them. They do not like to see their misery before they come into it; though perhaps, if they truly believed the sight of their coming misery, it might make them flee where the righteous flee and are safe. But, as I hinted before, because they shun even the thoughts of guilt and terror, when once they are rid of their awakenings about the terrors and wrath of God, they gladly harden their hearts, and choose such ways as will harden them more and more."

CHRISTIAN: *"You are pretty near the root of the issue, which is their lack of a true change of mind and will. They are therefore like the felon who quakes and trembles before the judge, and seems to repent most heartily; but the reason is his fear of the noose, not that he has any true remorse for his crime. This is evident, because, if you but let this man have his liberty, he will continue to be a thief and a rogue. Whereas, if his mind and heart were really changed, he would be far otherwise."*

HOPEFUL: *"I have shown you my reasons for their going back to their sinful course. Now, please show me the path of their backsliding."*

CHRISTIAN: *"So I will, gladly.*

They purposely draw off their thoughts from any remembrance of God, death, and the judgment to come.

Then by degrees, they cast off private religious duties, such as closet prayer, curbing their lusts, watching, sorrow for sin, and the like.

Then they shun the company of enthusiastic and fervent Christians.

After that, they grow cold in public religious duties, such as hearing the Word preached, reading the Word, godly fellowship, and the like.

Then they begin, as we say, to pick holes in the coats of some of the godly, trying to find some blemish in them. They do so devilishly, that they may have an excuse to throw religion behind their backs.

Then they begin to associate and join themselves with fleshly, immoral, and worldly men.

Then they give way to fleshly and immoral discourses in secret. They are glad if they can see such things in any who are reputed to be honest, for the example of these hypocrites emboldens them.

After this, they begin to openly play with little sins.

Being hardened, they then show themselves as they truly are.

"Thus, being launched again into the gulf of misery, they will everlastingly perish by their own deceptions, unless a miracle of grace prevents it."

CHAPTER 28

BEULAH LAND

Now I saw in my dream, that by this time the Pilgrims were now beyond the Enchanted Ground, and had entered into the country of Beulah, whose air was very sweet and pleasant. As their way went directly through Beulah Land, they delighted themselves there for a season. Yes, here they continually heard the singing of birds, and every day saw new flowers appear, and heard the song of the turtle-dove in the land. In this country the sun shines night and day. As it was beyond the Valley of the Shadow of Death, and also out of the reach of Giant Despair, they could not so much as see Doubting Castle.

Here they were within sight of the City they were traveling to. They also met some of the inhabitants of that City, for in this land the Shining Ones commonly walked, because it was upon the borders of Heaven.

In this land also, the contract between the Bride and the Bridegroom was renewed. Yes, here, 'As the Bridegroom rejoices over His Bride, so does their God rejoice over them.' Here they had no lack of grain or wine, for in this place they met with abundance of what they had sought for in all their pilgrimage. Here they heard voices from out of the City, loud voices, saying, 'Say to the daughter of Zion: Behold, your salvation comes! Behold, His reward is with Him!' Here all the inhabitants of the country called them, 'The holy people.' 'The redeemed of the Lord.' 'Sought out ones.'

Now, as they walked in this land, they rejoiced more than they had in all the former parts of their journey. Drawing near to the City, they had even a more perfect view of it. It was built of pearls and precious stones and the great street of the City was pure gold. So that by reason of the natural splendor of the City, and the reflection of the sunbeams upon it, Christian became lovesick with longing for it. Hopeful also had a fit or two of the same lovesickness. Therefore, they stayed here for a while, calling out, because of their longings, *"If you find my Beloved, tell Him that I am lovesick!"*

Now, being a little strengthened, and better able to bear their lovesickness, they walked on their way, and came yet nearer and nearer. They saw orchards, vineyards, and gardens and their gates opened into the highway. Now, as they came up to these places, behold, the gardener was standing there and the Pilgrims asked, *"Whose lovely vineyards and gardens are these?"*

The gardener answered, *"They are the King's, and are planted here for His own delight and also for the refreshment of Pilgrims."*

So the gardener brought them into the vineyards, and bid them to refresh themselves with the delicacies. He also showed them the King's walkways, and the arbors, where He delighted to be. So here they tarried and slept.

Now I beheld in my dream, that they talked more in their sleep at this time, than they ever did in all their journey.

As I was in deep thought about this, the gardener said to me: *"Why are you pondering the matter? It is the nature of the grapes of these vineyards to go down so sweetly, as to cause the lips of those who are asleep, to speak."*

So I saw that when the Pilgrims awoke, they prepared to go up to the City. But, as I said, the reflection of the sun upon the City, for 'the City was pure gold', was so resplendent, that they could not, as yet, behold it with open face, but only through an instrument made for that purpose.

So I saw, that as they went on, that two men, in clothing which shone like gold, met them. Their faces also shone as the light.

These men asked the Pilgrims where they came from and they told them. They also asked them where they had lodged, what difficulties and dangers, and what comforts and pleasures they met with along the way and they told them.

Then the men said, *"You have but two more difficulties to meet with and then you are in the City!"*

Christian and Hopeful asked the men to go along with them and they told them that they would.

"But," said they, *"you must obtain it by your own faith."*

So I saw in my dream that they went on together, until they came within sight of the gate of the City.

CHAPTER 29

THE RIVER OF DEATH

Now, I further saw, that between them and the gate was a river, but there was no bridge to pass over it, and the river was very deep. At the sight of this river, the Pilgrims were bewildered.

But the men said to them, *"You must go through the river, or you cannot enter in at the gate."*

The Pilgrims then began to inquire if there was any other way to the gate, to which the men answered, *"Yes, but only two since the foundation of the world have been permitted to tread that path, namely, Enoch and Elijah. Nor shall any others go that way until the last trumpet shall sound!"*

The Pilgrims then, especially Christian, began to lose heart. They looked this way and that, but they could find no way by which they might escape the river. Then they asked the men if the waters were all the same depth.

"No," they replied, *"You shall find it deeper or shallower, just as you believe in the King of the City."*

The Pilgrims then approached the water. Upon entering it, Christian began to sink! Crying out to his good friend Hopeful, he shouted, *"I am sinking in deep waters! The billows are rolling over my head, all His waves are washing over me!"*

Then Hopeful replied, *"Take courage, my brother, I feel the bottom, and it is firm!"*

Christian then cried out, *"Ah! my friend, the sorrows of death have compassed me about! I shall not see the land which flows with milk and honey!"*

With that, a great darkness and horror fell upon Christian, so that he could not see ahead of him. He also, in great measure, lost his senses, so that he could neither remember, nor talk coherently of any of those sweet refreshments which he had met with along the way of his pilgrimage. But all the words that he spoke still tended to manifest his horror of mind and heart-fears, that he would die in that river, and never obtain entrance at the gate.

Here also, as those two men who stood by perceived, Christian was much in troublesome thoughts concerning the sins that he had committed, both before and since he began to be a Pilgrim. It was also observed by his words, that he was troubled with apparitions of hobgoblins and evil spirits.

Hopeful, therefore, labored hard to keep his brother's head above water. Yes, sometimes Christian almost drowned, but then, in a short time, he would surface again, half dead.

Hopeful would also endeavor to encourage him, saying, *"Brother, I see the gate and men standing ready to receive us!"*

But Christian would answer, *"It is you, it is you they are waiting for! You have been Hopeful ever since I first knew you!"*

"And so have you," responded Hopeful.

"Ah, brother!" cried Christian, *"Surely if I were right with Him, then He would now arise to help me. Because of my sins, He has brought me into the snare, and has left me."*

Hopeful reminded him, *"My brother, you have quite forgotten the text where it is said of the wicked, 'They have no struggles in their death, but their strength is firm. They are not troubled as other men, neither are they plagued like other men.' These troubles and distresses that you are going through in these waters, are no indication that God has forsaken you. Rather, they are only sent to test you, as to whether you will call to mind what you have hitherto received of His goodness, and live upon Him in your present distresses."*

Then I saw in my dream, that Christian was in deep thought for a while.

Hopeful then added this word, *"Take courage, Jesus Christ makes you whole!"*

With that, Christian cried out with a loud voice, *"O! I see Him again, and He tells me, 'When you pass through the waters, I will be with you. When you go through the rivers, they shall not overflow you!'"*

Then they both took courage. After that, the enemy was as still as a stone, and could no longer hinder them. Christian therefore felt firm ground to stand upon and found that the rest of the river was but shallow. Thus they both crossed over the river.

CHAPTER 30

THE CELESTIAL CITY

Now, upon the bank of the river, on the other side, they saw the two Shining Men again, who were waiting for them. Therefore, having come out of the river, the Shining Men greeted them, saying, *"We are ministering spirits, sent forth to serve those who are heirs of salvation!"* Thus they went along together towards the gate.

Now that City stood upon a mighty hill, but the Pilgrims went up that hill with ease, because they had these two Shining Men to lead them up by their hands. Also, they left their mortal garments behind them in the river, for though they went in with them, they came out without them.

They, therefore, went up towards the City with much agility and speed, though the foundation upon which the City was framed, was higher than the clouds. They went up through the regions of the air, sweetly talking as they went, being comforted, because they had safely gotten over the river, and had such glorious companions to attend them.

The conversation they had with the Shining Ones was about the splendor of that place. They told the Pilgrims that the beauty and glory of it was inexpressible.

"There," said they, *"*is Mount Zion, the heavenly Jerusalem, the innumerable company of angels, and the spirits of just men made perfect! You are now going to the paradise of God, wherein you shall see the tree of life, and eat of its never-fading fruits! When you

arrive there, you shall have white robes given to you, and you shall walk and talk with the King every day, even through all the days of eternity!

"There you shall never again see such things as you saw when you were in the lower region of earth, namely, sorrow, sickness, affliction, and death, for the former things have passed away! You are now going to Abraham, to Isaac, and to Jacob, and to the prophets, men whom God has taken away from the evil to come, and who are now at rest, each one walking in his righteousness."

The Pilgrims then asked, *"What will we do in the holy City?"*

The Shining Ones answered, *"You will there receive the comforts of all your toil, and have joy for all your sorrow! You will reap what you have sown, even the fruit of all your prayers, and tears, and sufferings for the King along the way! In that place you will wear crowns of gold, and enjoy the perpetual sight and vision of the Holy One, for there you shall see Him as He is!*

"You shall also serve Him, whom you desired to serve while in the world, though with much difficulty because of the infirmity of your flesh. There you shall continually worship Him with praise, and shouting and thanksgiving! There your eyes shall be delighted with seeing Him and your ears with hearing the pleasant voice of the Mighty One!

"There you shall enjoy your friends again, who have gone there before you and you shall joyfully receive everyone who follows you into that holy place.

"There also, you shall be clothed with glory and majesty, fit to accompany the King of glory. When He shall come with trumpet sound in the clouds, as upon the wings of the wind, you shall come with Him! And when He shall sit upon the throne of judgment, you shall sit with Him. Yes, and when He shall pass sentence upon all the workers of iniquity, whether they are angels or men, you also shall have a voice in that judg-

ment, because they were both His and your enemies. And so you will be with the Lord forever!"

Now, while they were thus drawing towards the gate, behold a company of the heavenly hosts came out to meet them.

The two Shining Ones exclaimed, *"These are the men who have loved our Lord while they were in the world, and who have left all for His holy name. He has sent us to fetch them, and we have brought them thus far on their desired journey, that they may go in and look upon their Redeemer's face with joy!"*

Then the heavenly hosts gave a great shout, saying, *"Blessed are those who are invited to the marriage supper of the Lamb!"*

At this time, several of the King's trumpeters came out to meet them. They were arrayed in shining white clothing and with loud and melodious voices, they made even the heavens to echo with their sound. These trumpeters greeted Christian and Hopeful with ten thousand welcomes! This done, they surrounded the Pilgrims, so as to guard them through the upper regions, continually singing with melodious voices as they went, as if Heaven itself had come down to meet them!

Thus, therefore, they walked on together. As they walked, these trumpeters, with joyful sound, would always by mixing their music with pleasant looks and gestures, signify to Christian and Hopeful, how welcome they were in their company, and with what gladness they came to receive them.

Now Christian and Hopeful were as if in Heaven, before they came there, being swallowed up with the sight of angels, and with the hearing of their melodious voices. Here also they had the City itself fully in view, and they thought that they heard all the City bells ringing to welcome them in. But above all, they were encouraged by the warm and joyful thoughts of their own dwelling there, with such company and that forever and ever! O what tongue or pen could express their glorious joy! And thus they came up to the gate.

Now, there was written over the gate, in letters of gold, *"Blessed are those who obey His commandments, that they may have the right to the Tree of Life, and may enter through the gates into the City!"*

Then I saw in my dream, that the Shining Men bid them to call at the gate. And when they did, some looked over the gate, namely Enoch, Moses, Elijah and others, to whom it was told: *"These Pilgrims have come from the city of Destruction, for the love that they bear to the King of this place!"*

Then each Pilgrim handed in their certificate which they had received in the beginning of their journey. These certificates were carried to the King, who, when He had read them, said, *"Where are the men?"*

To whom it was answered, *"They are standing outside the gate."*

The King then commanded, *"Open the gates to all who are righteous, allow the faithful to enter in!"*

Now I saw in my dream that these two men went in at the gate. And behold! as they entered, they were transfigured, and they were arrayed with clothing which shone like gold. Some met them with harps and crowns, which were given to the Pilgrims. The harps were given for worship and the crowns were given as a token of honor.

Then I heard in my dream that all the bells in the City rang again for joy, and that it was said to the Pilgrims, *"Enter into the joy of your Lord!"*

I also heard Christian and Hopeful themselves singing with a loud voice, saying, *"Blessing, and honor, and glory, and power, be unto Him who sits upon the throne, and unto the Lamb, forever and ever!"*

Now just as the gates were opened to let the men in, I looked in after them and, behold, the City shone like the sun! The streets also were paved with gold, and on them walked many men, with crowns on their heads, palms in their hands, and golden harps to sing praises with! There were also some angelic beings with wings, and they sang back and forth without intermission, *"Holy, holy, holy, is the Lord!"* After that, they closed up the gates. When I had seen all of this, I wished that I myself was among them.

Now while I was gazing upon all these things, I turned my head to look back, and saw Ignorance come up to the river side. He soon got over the river, and without half of the difficulty which Christian and Hopeful met with. For it happened that one called Vain-hope, a ferryman, was there and with his boat he helped Ignorance cross the river.

Then I saw that Ignorance ascended the hill, and came up to the gate all alone. There was no man to meet him with the least encouragement. When he arrived at the gate, he looked up to the writing that was above it, and then began to knock, supposing that entrance would quickly be given to him. But he was asked by the men who looked over the top of the gate, *"Where have you come from? What do you want?"*

He answered them, *"I have eaten and drank in the presence of the King and He has taught in our streets!"*

Then they asked him for his certificate, that they might go in and show it to the King. So he fumbled in his bosom for one, but found none.

Then they asked, *"Have you no certificate?"*

But the man answered not a word.

So they told the King about Ignorance, but He would not go down to see him. Instead He commanded the two Shining Ones who had conducted Christian and Hopeful to the City, to go out and take Ignorance, bind him hand and foot, and cast him away.

So they took Ignorance up, and carried him through the air, to the door which I had seen in the side of the hill and threw him in there!

Then I saw that there was a way to Hell, even from the very gates of Heaven, as well as from the city of Destruction!

So I awoke, and behold, it was a dream!

Next to the Bible, the book that I value most is John Bunyan's Pilgrim's Progress. I believe I have read it through at least a hundred times! It is a volume of which I never seem to tire; and the secret of its freshness is that it is so largely compiled from the Scriptures. It is really Biblical teaching put into the form of a simple yet very striking allegory. – Charles Spurgeon

This book has been edited into modern English by Grace Gems. A treasury of ageless, sovereign grace, devotional writings, Grace Gems is the largest free archive of classic Sovereign Grace devotional books, sermons, quotes, audio and video on the internet.

www.GraceGems.org